Israeli Masculinity, Sex Work, Consumerism

Israeli Masculinity, Sex Work, and Consumerism: Heteronormativity and Sexual Repertoires explores the inner world of Israeli sex work consumers and their use of digital technologies on which intense feelings of social togetherness and belonging create a localized form of homosociality and brotherhood.

The first of its kind to offer an in-depth analysis of masculine sexual repertoires in the field of sex consumption, this book uses extensive data and observations of online ethnography among a community of Israeli sex consumers operating online. It elucidates the economics of demand in the field of sexual consumption and highlights how the rise of the thriving online communities of sex consumers can function as a platform on which power relations between men themselves are publicly displayed and are constantly challenged.

Israeli Masculinity, Sex Work, and Consumerism: Heteronormativity and Sexual Repertoires will be suitable for researchers in Gender and Sexuality Studies, Sociology, Anthropology and Criminology.

Yeela Lahav-Raz is a senior lecturer at the Department of Sociology and Anthropology at the Ben-Gurion University of the Negev, Israel. She is an anthropologist specializing in gender and sexuality, sex work studies, digital anthropology and the intersections of gender and sexual politics, digital technology, and marginalized communities.

Focus on Global Gender and Sexuality

Israeli Masculinity, Sex Work, and Consumerism

Heteronormativity and Sexual Repertoires

Yeela Lahav-Raz

Routledge
Taylor & Francis Group

LONDON AND NEW YORK

First published 2024
by Routledge
4 Park Square, Milton Park, Abingdon, Oxon OX14 4RN

and by Routledge
605 Third Avenue, New York, NY 10158

Routledge is an imprint of the Taylor & Francis Group, an informa business

British Library Cataloguing-in-Publication Data
A catalogue record for this book is available from the British Library

Library of Congress Cataloging-in-Publication Data
Names: Lahav-Raz, Yeela, author.
Title: Israeli masculinity, sex work, and consumerism: heteronormativity and sexual repertoires / Yeela Lahav-Raz.
Description: Abingdon, Oxon; New York, NY: Routledge, 2023. |
Series: Focus on global gender and sexuality |
Includes bibliographical references and index. | Contents: Introduction: The Consumption of Sex in the Digital Age – The Consumer Sexual Script – The Hunter Sexual Script – The Addict Sexual Script – Moving Beyond the "Client." |
Identifiers: LCCN 2023034309 (print) | LCCN 2023034310 (ebook) |
Subjects: LCSH: Men–Sexual behavior–Israel. | Masculinity–Israel. | Heterosexism–Israel. | Sex industry–Social aspects–Israel. | Online social networks–Israel.
Classification: LCC HQ1090.7.I75 L34 2023 (print) |
LCC HQ1090.7.I75 (ebook) | DDC 306.70811095694–dc23/eng/20230819
LC record available at https://lccn.loc.gov/2023034309
LC ebook record available at https://lccn.loc.gov/2023034310

ISBN: 9780367652715 (hbk)
ISBN: 9780367652722 (pbk)
ISBN: 9781003128670 (ebk)

DOI: 10.4324/9781003128670

Typeset in Times New Roman
by Deanta Global Publishing Services, Chennai, India

Contents

Preface

In October 2010, as part of what I thought at the time would become my doctoral thesis, I began an ethnographic research project on youth and young adults involved in commercial sex. As part of my fieldwork, I joined ELEM (Youth in Distress), a nonprofit Israeli organization dedicated to treating and transforming the lives of troubled youth. One of ELEM's projects is Outreach Vans, which are specially equipped vans providing immediate responses to youth at risk on the streets. At the time, a central location for the vans was Tel Aviv's old central bus station, where there was an active street sex work scene. After one of my visits, I wrote in my field diary:

> I'm walking in the streets of Tel Aviv toward ELEM's van, already parked at the central bus station. During my walk from the city center to its southern streets, the atmosphere, sights, and smells are starting to change. Walking by myself alone at this time of night, I become vigilant. There are only men, most of them refugees and asylum seekers; some are alone, others scattered in groups, drinking in deserted parking lots. I'm trying to walk without making eye contact; the eye sees everything, but the gaze is directed far away. In my head echoes an Israeli song called "Brooklyn" which portrays Brooklyn's axis – the holy and the profane. It's the same in Tel Aviv, where there is a combination of the upper, visible city and lower Tel Aviv, the one hidden from the public eye... I reach the van. We are headed to Mount Zion St., a popular venue for street sex workers. We are working our routine: getting the chairs out, offering something to drink and eat, and handing out condoms. I'm looking around; there are only men of varied appearance and age. Most of them are driving their cars slowly; their heads lean forward, scanning the area. Some have baby seats in the back seat; some have high-tech company stickers on their car. It's midnight: why aren't they at home? What are they looking for? Where are they running away from, and who are they running away from? Dozens of wandering and abandoned men.

Two years of fieldwork with youth and young adults familiarized me with how they connect with their clients. Most of the youth I met used social network sites such as Facebook, Tinder, LGBTQ online dating apps, WhatsApp, and sex websites. The exception was an online portal used by youth to read consumers' reports about their sexual performances. While the social networks and websites offered an intermediate arena, the sex portal contained, among other things, a thriving online community of sex consumers sharing their sexual experiences. The more exposed I was to the hidden world behind the screen, the more it drew me in. The experiences I gained from the two years of fieldwork on the streets and the research wasteland at the time regarding Israeli sex work consumers launched my long journey of understanding the inner world of Israeli sex work consumers and their use of digital technologies as a platform on which intense feelings of social togetherness and belonging create a localized form of homosociality and brotherhood.

Book Outline

The opening chapter introduces the reader to the emerging worldwide research on sexual consumption. It begins with an outline of sex-buying patterns and particular segments of the industry from the clients' perspectives. This includes a focus on one of the major aspects of commercial sexual services: digital technologies and their huge impact on the rearrangement of modern-day sexual consumption and production. Emphasis is placed on how client review sites have become a space where a localized form of homosociality and brotherhood is created. The second sub-chapter goes on to reexamine Gagnon and Simon's (1973) sexual script theory as a springboard for the discussion on the consumption of sex in the digital age and the construction of Israeli masculine repertoires. It thus moves beyond simplistic and derogatory understandings of "the client" as a heuristic category. Finally, the third sub-chapter introduces the reader to the main characteristics of the Israeli sex industry.

Chapter 2 introduces the sexual script of Israeli sex consumers. By placing a particular emphasis on consumer culture, the chapter shows how Israeli sex consumers adopt, understand, and implement consumer culture ideals in their sex-buying experiences. These experiences are embedded in constant moral boundary work, which aims to avoid being a *freier* (Hebrew slang for a "sucker") – one of Israeli society's central cultural motifs. The chapter thus sheds light on how consumer economic rationality interweaves with current local consumption patterns in the sex industry. Furthermore, it demonstrates how consumer cultural rationalization shapes personal and emotional relationships not only with the woman with whom the sexual act is performed but primarily with the male community that participates in the sexual recreation.

Chapter 3 continues the examination of Israeli sex consumers' sexual scripts by presenting the sexual script of the "hunter." This chapter's main focal point stresses that this sexual script is a mixture of intersecting characteristics from the universal dominant repertoire of hegemonic, heteronormative hyper-masculinity and Israeli masculine hegemonic ideals of militarized masculinity. This focus on Israeli manhood and its hegemonic cultural components demonstrates how the sexual script of the hunter functions as a performative and theatrical platform on which to play out an imagined masculinity where the consumption of paid sex serves as a socio-erotic liminoid ritual that is both relational and pleasurable.

Chapter 4 explores the sexual script of the "addict" as an elaborating symbol of victimhood. The chapter's specific emphasis on clients who self-identify as addicts present this sexual script as a manifestation of hybrid masculinity that enables sex consumers to maneuver selectively between hegemonic and counter-hegemonic performances. This maneuvering is accomplished by combining two discourses of the self: the discourse of the neoliberal, psychologized, and private self located in therapeutic logic and the discourse of the national and political-collective self located in the emotional character of Israeli victim culture. The chapter shows how the sexual script of the addict becomes both a coping and a compensation strategy, enabling clients to resist stigmatization as exploiters while sheltering under the protective shadow of the addict label.

The final chapter brings together the previous chapters' findings on how various cultural logics intertwine with the sexual scripts of Israeli sex consumers. It explores the way in which moving away from a view of scripts as a given set of rules enables us to uncover the processes through which scripts are reproduced and negotiated. They thus become what Boltanski and Thévenot (1999, 2006) called moral justification regimes within which they operate when discussing their experiences and involvement in commercial sex. By moving beyond sexual script typologies, the concluding chapter shows the various cultural repertoires of homosociality that drive the book's three sexual scripts, which have become a toolkit of habits, skills, and styles from which people construct action strategies. It thus offers a nuanced perspective on the rigid notion of "masculinities," opting for a more flexible terrain of situated social practice, according to which the three scripts are flexible, pragmatic, and accessible to consumers in different contexts. Furthermore, the concluding chapter develops a new theoretical concept of "communitext": a combination of Turner's (1969) concept of communitas, which denotes intense feelings of social togetherness and belonging, and the emphasis the community places on writing sexual experiences online. This new concept of "communitext" reflects how sex consumers' online communities create a localized and situationally constructed form of homosociality. It thus contributes both theoretical and empirical perspectives to the broad discussions of paying for sex in the digital age and the construction of masculinity as a homosocial rite of passage.

1 Introduction

The Consumption of Sex in the Digital Age

Sex Buying Patterns

Masculinity is anchored in the power men exert over women and among themselves. In his attempt to understand the "deep structure of masculinity," Gilmore (1990, 1997) pointed out that masculinity is not a natural state that occurs spontaneously during biological maturation but rather an uncertain and precarious prize to be won or wrested through struggle. While masculinity is not a fixed term, and different cultures can vary its meaning at different times, cultures with nothing in common share the same obsessive quest to validate masculinity. Furthermore, one's masculinity is constantly questioned and must be proved continuously. It relies on rigid codes that require decisive action in different spheres of life: a husband, a father, a son, a lover, and a financial provider. A central part of this identity work requires adopting collective practices concerning the many different arenas of life, among which, of course, is the sexual arena.

Through gender training or what Gilmore called "dramatic acting" (1990, p. 12), men learn to perform masculinity convincingly; instead of expressing fear or pain, they are pushed into competitiveness and emotional opacity. They learn to stifle any expression of intimacy and to express constant sexual desire for (multiple) women. Women, in this process, thus symbolize the heterosexual dimension of men. Failure in any of the collective practices mentioned may lead to feelings of shame, guilt, and anxiety, making masculinity the site of constant examination and an arena dominated by the fear of performance failure. As a result, a man's ability to function sexually is also closely related to social perceptions of masculinity as a demonstrative test of courage and achievement through which the individual acquires his masculinity in front of the entire male community. Understanding masculinity as a rite of passage may explain why the consumption of commercial sex has, for centuries, been considered a manhood act of performing hegemonic masculinity and marked men as "normal."

However, society's double-binding perception of men as deviant, sick, addicted, pathological, and violent (Hammond, 2015; Huschke & Schubotz, 2016; Lim & Cheah, 2020; Neal, 2018) teaches them to cloak their actions in silence, secrecy, and shame (Kong, 2016) and, hence, to neutralize or normalize

DOI: 10.4324/9781003128670-1

them (Lim & Cheah, 2020). Thus, while the meanings ascribed to buying and selling sex have tended to change according to the social, cultural, and historical processes in which transactions are located (Agustin, 2008; Brents & Hausbeck, 2007), sex work remains highly stigmatized in most societies (Milrod & Monto, 2012; Sanders, 2018; Weitzer, 2018). The silence resulting from these polarized but complementary perceptions, ranging from normalization to condemnation, turns sex consumption into a "sexual closet." In the face of their "spoiled" identity (Goffman, 1963), sex consumers engage in different edgework skills, such as passing, covering, time management, compartmentalization, and denial, in an attempt to maintain the boundary of secrecy and disclosure between a public "good man" and a private "bad guy" (Sanders, 2013).

Despite sex consumption being a "sexual closet," the question of what men buy when they pay for sexual encounters has been the subject of extensive debate over the past few decades. This debate often results from two equally extreme and reductionist conceptual and ideological frameworks. The first is radical feminism, which finds any kind of sex work, and often even sexuality itself, inherently and irrevocably exploitative within the patriarchy (Echols, 2016). Paying for sex is therefore perceived as a deviant behavior resulting from personal pathology or unjust and exploitative patriarchal power relations (Coy et al., 2019; O'Connell-Davidson, 1998). The second framework is sex-positive feminism, which highlights the voluntary exchange of money for sex (Birch, 2015; Monto & McRee, 2005; Sanders, 2008) and therefore supports the right of sex workers to perform erotic labor and calls for destigmatization of all parties involved in the industry, including consumers. This debate has created a polarized discussion in which sex work is perceived as either oppressive or liberating, and sex workers are either striving for pleasure or subject to danger. This polarization shapes and is clearly reflected in attitudes toward sex consumers.

In the context of widespread criminalization, pathologization, and normalization, vast scholarly attention has therefore been paid to understanding client typologies and their motivations for buying commercial sex, resulting in a wide range of findings (see Bertone & Ferrero Camoletto, 2019 for a review). Regarding client characteristics, some studies have indicated that sex buying is most prevalent among White, middle-aged or older, unmarried or unhappily married men who hold liberal sexual attitudes and have had many unpaid sexual partners (Della Giusta et al., 2017a; Kotsadam & Jakobsson, 2011; Milrod & Monto, 2017; Monto, 2000; Monto & McRee, 2005; Ompad et al., 2013; Pitts et al., 2004; Rissel et al., 2017; Ward et al., 2005). Others, in contrast, have found that sex consumers constitute a heterogeneous group composed of all ages, ethnicities, social classes, marital statuses, and professions (Birch, 2015; Monto & Milrod, 2014; Peled et al., 2020; Sanders et al., 2017).

There is, however, widespread agreement on the complex intertwining of motivations in clients' accounts and their situational and life course variability (Frank, 2005; Peng, 2007; Sanders, 2013). These motivations may include a search for satisfying sexual desires or fantasies (Huysamen, 2020), thrill-seeking (Lahav-Raz, 2020a), physical closeness, and the desire for emotional disclosure in the name of a "girlfriend experience" (Huff, 2011; Milrod & Monto, 2012; Milrod & Weitzer, 2012; Pitts et al., 2004; Sanders, 2013; Weitzer, 2009). Some studies have highlighted biological and normative sexual urges related to dominant heteronormative masculine scripts about sexuality and identity (Brooks-Gordon, 2006; Coy et al., 2019; Hammond & van Hooff, 2020; Huysamen & Boonzaier, 2015; Kong, 2015; Marttila, 2008; Prior & Peled, 2019; Sanders, 2008). Others have shown how patterns of sex-buying behavior differ across contexts, specifically indoor versus outdoor sex venues (Sanders, 2013; Weitzer, 2009).

Another key theme in the literature about consumerism and sex commerce concerns emotional intimacy as a critical component of the commercial exchange; intimacy is thus not exempt from the commercial sexual experience but rather integrated within it (Bernstein, 2001, 2007; Huysamen & Boonzaier, 2015; Jones & Hannem, 2018; Katsulis, 2010; Milrod & Weitzer, 2012; Sanders, 2013; Zheng, 2006). The blurring of boundaries between commercial transactions and social relationships (Huff, 2011; Sanders, 2013) provides a useful lens through which to understand both the complexities and meanings associated with buying sexual services, specifically physical sexual acts and emotional intimacy (Huysamen & Boonzaier, 2015). The commodification of intimacy and the emotional aspects of the client–sex worker relationship led Sanders (2008) to claim that the stories of men who buy sex are not only about sexual relationships; they are also social stories about how their sexuality merges with other parts of their lives and their needs, desires, and roles. These various and sometimes conflicting findings make it difficult to fully understand who the client "really" is, his characteristics, and his motivations.

Sex work encounters are complex economic transactions mediated by various cultural practices, including new media technologies (Pettinger, 2015; Sanders et al., 2020). Digital technologies have profoundly impacted many aspects of people's work and social lives, including the buying and selling of sexual services (Cunningham et al., 2017). Hence, to understand current sexual repertoires and patterns in sex commerce, it should be remembered that most sex commerce is now mediated by or provided through digital technologies such as email, chat rooms, social media platforms, and apps, phones, and webcams (Sanders et al., 2016). The emergent cyberspace enables various sex commerce possibilities for both sex workers and their clients (Pajnik et al., 2016; Sanders et al., 2016; Weitzer, 2013), with positive and negative results.

Alongside adverse outcomes such as violence, online harassment, and stalking (Davies & Evans, 2007; Hughes, 2004), researchers focusing on sex work as a form of labor have highlighted how cyberspace offers sex workers new opportunities to market their services, provides peer support and professional networking, increases their independence and autonomy, and thus creates a safer and more lucrative context of sex work (Cunningham et al., 2017; Pajnik et al., 2016; Sanders, 2005; Sanders et al., 2018). However, the migration to online platforms and services has also focused research attention on the creation of thriving online communities where clients can share their sexual experiences via online review forums (Castle & Lee, 2008; Earle & Sharp, 2008, 2016; Holt & Blevins, 2007; Holt et al., 2008; Milrod & Monto, 2012; Sanders, 2013; Shumka et al., 2017). As Sanders et al. (2018) demonstrated, client review forums function as online spaces where clients post messages about their experiences of buying sexual services, including reviews of individual sex workers.

While Boyd (2008) presented the general weakening of online forums and communities in favor of emerging social networks where the individual has a visible identity, sex consumers' online communities have maintained their popularity since they offer inherent anonymity. Furthermore, unlike other digital platforms, they enable sex consumers a deep and ongoing sharing of their sexual experiences. Despite having always been a male rite of passage, sexual consumption has remained a largely solitary experience; men did not share their sexual experiences due to prohibitions surrounding the issue and the associated stigma. Sex consumers' online communities are still flourishing as they offer an anonymous liberated arena where "men can be men" and can shape their collective masculine identity.

Various issues have been studied concerning the involvement of consumers in online forums. These include studies on the instrumental information that consumers share (Castle & Lee, 2008; Holt & Blevins, 2007; Horswill & Weitzer, 2018; Joseph & Black, 2012; Soothill & Sanders, 2005; Tylera & Jovanovski, 2018) and client engagement in emotional management when buying sex (Milrod & Weitzer, 2012). Some have considered sex consumers' use of online spaces to solicit recommendations (Holt & Blevins, 2007; Holt et al., 2008) and client forums' reinforcement of ideas about heterosexuality, hegemonic masculinity, and fraternity (Lahav-Raz, 2020a). According to Shumka et al. (2017), sex consumers participating in online forum discussions often exaggerate their claims of hegemonic masculinity, thus preserving the typically homosocial environments within which men are tacitly expected to sexualize and objectify women; consumers who participate in online communities are, however, only a fraction of the overall customer base (Sanders et al., 2020).

Moreover, sex consumers are influenced by underlying assumptions about how consumers wish to be seen by other consumers and accepted norms of interactions within a community of sex consumers. Thus, unlike other platforms where sex consumers operate, online communities, as a unique platform focusing on writing about sexual experiences, enable sex consumers to learn about themselves by sharing the commonalities of their sexual experiences and establishing reciprocal emotional connections with their peers. These communities thus become a platform through which sexual scripts of localized and universal forms of homosociality and brotherhood repertoires are created.

The Sexual Script Theory

Connell's (1995) and Connell and Messerscmidt's (2005) theorization of masculinity patterns and their various configurations – "hegemonic," "complicit," "marginal," and "subordinate" – have inspired researchers to examine both the commonalities and the lack of computability and inherent tensions and resistance facing sex consumers in light of dominant hegemonic masculinities. Several studies have therefore focused on masculine repertories that reproduce and reinforce (universal) patriarchal, heteronormative discourses which are intrinsic to sex consumers' male identity (Colosi, 2020; Hammond & van Hooff, 2020; Huysamen & Boonzaier, 2018; Sanders, 2008; Shumka et al., 2017; Vaughn, 2019). Some researchers have also looked at patterns of consumer masculinity reinforcing heteronormative male identity (Huysamen & Boonzaier, 2015; Lahav-Raz, 2019; Pettinger, 2013, 2015), which enable consumers' attempts to maximize their gain. Others, however, have highlighted manifestations of fragile masculinity (Joseph & Black, 2012) or expressions of vulnerability, loneliness, and insecurity in the process of buying sex (Birch, 2015; Frank, 2003; Jones & Hannem, 2018; Joseph & Black, 2012; Kong, 2016; Lahav-Raz, 2022; Peng, 2007; Prior & Peled, 2019; Sanders, 2008).

These multifaceted masculine configurations indicate how masculinity within sex commerce can be fluid and context-specific (Colosi, 2020; Prior, 2022). Nonetheless, there is wide agreement among researchers that the consumption of commercial sex and sex venues can become gender training arenas where men can construct and practice complex matrixes of heteronormative masculinity (Frank, 2003; Kong, 2015; Mbonye et al., 2022; Prior & Peled, 2021). Furthermore, in a recent interpretive qualitative meta-synthesis about the identity construction of men who pay women for sex, Prior and Peled (2021) showed the discourse of masculinity to be the most prevalent of all the social discourses setting the stage for identity construction processes among sex consumers. Sex consumers' diverse experiences are, accordingly, gendered, sexual, intimate, consumerist, and related to power relations and social stigma. All of these experiences are connected to masculine identity construction, which turns masculinity into a metadiscourse in the identity construction processes of these men. Masculinity within sex consumption thereby becomes a set of social practices, and, as Colosi (2020) demonstrated, men can enact different versions of masculinity in diverse social spaces and situations.

Alongside these attempts to refigure different forms of masculinity and its centrality to the discourse on sex consumption, Bertone and Ferrero Camoletto (2019) highlighted the paucity of literature using the "male sexual scripts" framework. While Gagnon and Simon's (1973) theory of sexual scripts became seminal for understanding human sexual activity as social and learned interactions, there has been little attempt to apply it to patterns of sex consumption (Bertone & Ferrero Camoletto, 2019). In light of this research gap, the conceptualization of sex buying as a scripting practice of both local and universal heteronormative masculine sexual scripts can be a valuable perspective for addressing the complex, dynamic, and situational construction of the meanings of sex consumption, which move beyond simplistic and derogatory understandings of "the client" as a heuristic category. Hence, using the interactionist perspective on sexual scripting developed by Gagnon and Simon (1973) highlights the dominance of specific heteronormative practices of sexual scripts. It also recognizes the mechanisms through which sexual scripts are reproduced and can be negotiated and questioned within broader universal and local changing configurations of gender and sexuality.

According to Gagnon (1990), a sexual script is an organized cognitive schema used to recognize a situation as sexual, name the actors involved, and plot their behavior. While the sexual script defines the space, time, identity, and content of the sexual encounter, it is not a fixed set of instructions but rather a dynamic and multidimensional process. Simon and Gagnon (1986) showed the reflexive and interpretive processes of scripting to contain three interwoven dimensions: cultural, interpersonal, and intrapsychic. The cultural scenarios are linked to different historical periods and social changes: sexual scripts provide instructional guides for defining the boundaries of what is sexual and making sense of individual experiences as sexual at a given time. These cultural norms and values influence both interpersonal and intrapsychic scripts. In the interpersonal scenario, sexual scripts draw on shared symbols and cultural expectations about sex and sexuality to permit individuals to interact and play out a "scene" without explicitly discussing the interaction's parameters. Finally, in the intrapsychic scenario, sexual scripts define the motivational elements that produce arousal or, at least, a commitment to a behavioral sequence and give meaning to this behavior.

Sexual script theory guides how the individual should feel and behave (Burghart, 2018), and sexual scripts are thus organized according to gender, class, ethnicity, and other social vectors. They determine an individual's choice of sexual actions and their subsequent qualitative experience. As such, much attention has been given to gender differences regarding cultural, social, and sexual scripts. There is a double standard in the traditional heterosexual sexual script, which endorses different sexual behavior for women and men: masculine gender roles have long dictated power, independence, assertiveness, sexual abundance, and exploration as the typically hegemonic masculine ideals; women, on the other hand, are expected to confine their sexual behavior to the context of a committed relationship.

While sexual scripts provide guidelines for the "appropriate" sexual behavior and sexual encounters learned through culture and the interactions of others, the sexual script theory has attracted little attention among sex consumer researchers. To date, the most profound application of the sexual script theory to sex consumption are Sanders' (2008, 2013) studies on the commonalities between the sexual scripts men enact as clients and a more traditional heterosexual male sexual script. Based mainly on an analysis of written biographies and interviews with men who pay for sex, Sanders demonstrated that the sexual script of male clients in commercial sexual relationships does not significantly differ from that of heterosexual men in conventional relationships. According to her findings, clients tend to draw upon scripts around emotional intimacy and relational involvement with sex workers to frame their experiences. Saunders thus challenged the perception of sex consumption as an exceptional or exclusive sexual script and questioned the perceived boundaries between commercial and impersonal sex.

Inspired by Sanders, others have tried to further explore various manifestations of sex consumers' sexual scripts. For example, Jones and Hannem (2018) focused on clients' intrapsychic scripts, arguing that previous typologies of client behavior ignore the role of intimacy and the meaning individuals ascribe to their own experiences and actions. Their findings highlight male sex consumers' search for the appropriate cultural script concerning pursuing sexual interaction with (often multiple) desirable women. At the same time, the findings violate scripts of romantic sexuality, which suggests that such encounters should be organic, rooted in mutual desire, and free of (explicit) commodification. The authors thus claim that sex workers and clients construct interactions that draw on these dominant cultural scripts, rewriting the script to set the boundaries of the encounter and allowing clients to experience intimacy within a bounded temporal and emotional frame.

Another example is Bertone and Ferrero Camoletto's (2019) study of sexual biographies of middle-aged and elderly men, highlighting the dimension of temporality as part of the scripting process. While their main focus was not on buying sex but rather on men's sexual biographies, Bertone and Ferrero Camoletto showed that the sexual script, which unfolds over time, entails an ongoing reinterpretation of one's sexual experiences to make sense of one's biography. Clients' interpretations of their involvement in paying for sex are therefore constructed alongside other trajectories over their life course. Similar to Jones and Hannem (2018), Bertone and Ferrero Camoletto (2019) found that sex consumers rescripted their experiences to achieve biographical consistency under new terms.

The examples presented thus far were based primarily on interviews with men who pay for sex, and they reinforce evidence from previous studies on the identification of continuity between interactions in commercial sex and those relationships conventionally defined as non-commercial (Milrod & Monto, 2012), and the relations between changing experiences of buying sexual services and more general changes in practices of intimacy and sexuality (Bernstein, 2007). In contrast to these studies, the following chapters concentrate on the various sexual scripts of Israeli sex consumers participating in online communities. A focus on the online community of sex consumers allows for a richer corpus than a limited sample of interviewees and a comprehensive understanding of the negotiation of sexual scripts in different indoor and outdoor sex venues. It also fosters an awareness of the close relationship between the sexual script and digital technology, which facilitates and mediates most of contemporary sex commerce.

The following chapters attempt to answer Bertone and Ferrero Camoletto's (2019) call for a deeper exploration of how people do gender by scripting their sexual experiences. Rather than investigating which sexual scripts are available to which men in which situations, the chapters aim to explore the mechanisms through which sexual scripts are reproduced and can be negotiated, questioned, and changed. As Masters et al. (2013) argued, dominant cultural scripts are not a given but rather require maintenance and reinforcement at personal and dyadic levels. As will be shown, the various sexual scripts of Israeli sex consumers become repertories of what Boltanski and Thévenot (1999, 2006) called "moral justification regimes," within which sex consumers operate when discussing their experiences and involvement in commercial sex. According to Boltanski and Thevenot's pragmatic morality (2006), perceptions and practices depend on context: some rationales and values have meaning in one context, while others acquire meaning in other contexts. Within the context, individuals adopt different frameworks of moral reasoning, known as "justification regimes," which operate as logic platforms. When a given sexual script becomes a justification regime, it becomes a resource for a meaning-making "toolkit" (Swidler, 1986), enabling sex consumers to make sense of their experiences, themselves, and others. Furthermore, the different sexual scripts express different moral logics in different situations to direct sex consumers' actions, arguments, and agreements within contrasting sex venues. The flexible switching between different sexual scripts and justification regimes enables us to understand how sex consumers define themselves and their activities and to navigate between various cultural logics in the context of moral taint and stigma.

To understand how distinct universal and local articulations of masculinity inform the structure, organization, understanding, and experience of Israeli sex consumers, it is vital to first address key sociological issues concerning Israeli masculinity.

Key Sociological Issues in Israeli Masculinity

While the different chapters of this book will emphasize distinct elements concerning Israeli masculinity, it is important to present key sociological issues relating to the existing research about Israeli masculinity.

Israeli society was born out of rejection of the image of the Diaspora Jew man, characterized negatively through his appearance, language, culture, and range of occupations as weak, inferior, feminine, and an object of ridicule (Boyarin, 1997; Gluzman, 1997; Kamir, 2011). Many scholars have addressed the characteristics of the "New Jew" as the Israeli counter model of this perception, such as the willingness for self-sacrifice, the aversion to formalities in dress, speech, or behavior, straightforwardness almost to the point of rudeness, and the strong, brave fighter with a muscular, rough, unkempt, and careless appearance (Bloch & Lemish, 2005; Hirsch & Grosswirth Kachtan, 2018; Katriel, 1986; Roniger & Feige, 1992; Seltenreich, 2009). The Zionist ideal of the "Halutz" (pioneer) thus became the emerging society's key symbol: he who conquered the land by physical labor created, in doing so, a highly masculinized New Jew.

Furthermore, the early Zionist construction of masculinity was accompanied by the militarization of Israeli society. Since Israeli society has, since the outset, faced serious military confrontations, pioneering and military discourses are closely linked with the formation of quests for courage, adventure, and heroism as Israeli masculine ideals (Hirsch & Grosswirth Kachtan, 2018; Sasson-Levy 2002, 2008). According to Sasson-Levy (2008), the Israeli military experience has created a militaristic culture in which camaraderie, sociability, and self-sacrifice are significant motifs, and lifelong relationships flourish regardless of social or political differences. The achievement of the hegemonic masculinity status of the Jewish combat soldier has attracted the attention of most Israeli researchers of masculinity, who have examined various aspects concerning the associations between military service, masculinity, and citizenship (Ben-Ari & Levi-Schreiber, 2000; Israeli & Rosman-Stollman, 2015; Kaplan, 2003, 2008; Kepten, 2023; Sasson-Levy, 2002, 2003, 2008; Spector-Mersel & Gilbar, 2021). Others have highlighted additional components of the hegemonic soldier conceptual framework, such as ethno-gendered resistance strategies (Kachtan & Wasserman, 2015; Lomsky-Feder & Rapoport, 2003; Sion & Ben-Ari, 2009) and the ways in which men undo and redo gender to reproduce their supremacy and create a new and "improved" form of masculinity (Wasserman et al., 2018).

The military arena maintains its hegemony, and the combat soldier has remained one of the principal values of this hegemonic masculinity, endorsed by the community and the state. However, the move in Israeli culture toward a liberal-capitalist economic perspective that has led to a more individualistic and materialistic outlook (Roniger & Feige, 1992) has shifted research attention to other aspects of Israeli masculinity. Studies have, for example, focused on a new masculinity ideology rooted in the therapeutic discourse of Israeli men (Kaplan, 2007; Kaplan & Knoll, 2019) and the impact of masculinity on perceptions of fatherhood (Offer & Kaplan, 2021) and consumerism (Rosenmann et al., 2018). Others have highlighted the deep crisis of masculinity, especially among marginalized communities (Birenbaum-Carmeli & Inhorn, 2009; Hakak, 2009; Monterescu, 2003; Sa'ar & Yahia-Younis, 2008), while recent studies have explored Israeli men's construction of male images and practices in the sports arena (Hertzog & Lev, 2019; Levy et al., 2016).

The literature presented thus far shows how Israeli researchers have emphasized the relationship between masculinity ideals and various social issues such as militarism, citizenship, class, immigration, and ethnicity, among others. There is, however, a lack of research on the intersections between Israeli masculine components and their impact on sexual buying patterns. Only in recent years have researchers started to explore the experiences of Israeli men who pay for sex either in Israel or abroad (Bruker & Sa'ar, 2019; Lahav-Raz, 2019, 2020a, 2022; Lahav-Raz et al., 2023; Prior, 2022; Prior & Peled, 2019, 2021, 2022; Tal-Hadar et al., 2022). However, most of these studies found similar themes to other international studies and disregarded the potential impact of the Israeli context on their findings. Since masculine qualities have long been valued as an organizing principle in the deep structure of Israeli society, this book aims to fill this gap by showing how various repertoires of masculinity characterize Israeli sex consumers operating online.

Before introducing the book's empirical study, the following sub-chapter provides a review of the recent legal developments and sociocultural perceptions relating to the governance of the Israeli sex industry.

The Israeli Sex Industry

The twenty-first century has seen renewed attention to prostitution and sexual commerce. According to Sanders et al. (2020), the global politics of borders and its concern with gender inequality and human rights have affected recent trends in commercial sex policies, according to which different groups battle out the best way to govern sex in the modern age. One of the leading policies receiving considerable support over the last two decades is the End Demand approach, which, based on neo-abolitionist feminism, views sex work as a form of violence against women and inherently degrading, harmful, and exploitative (Oselin & Weitzer, 2013). This neo-abolitionist model, pioneered by Sweden in 1999, criminalizes sex consumers and is purported to remove all laws that criminalize female sex workers. Intending to minimize gender inequality, it shifts the focus from the sellers to those now perceived as perpetrators (Halley et al., 2006; Harrington, 2018; Sanders et al., 2020; Vuolajärvi, 2019; Waltman, 2011). The Swedish neo-abolitionist law has evolved into a global "supermodel" for prostitution policy (Hammond, 2015; Kingston & Thomas, 2019; McGarry & FitzGerald, 2018; Sanders & Campbell, 2014), and laws to criminalize clients have subsequently been passed in Iceland (2009), Norway (2009), Canada (2014), France (2015), Northern Ireland (2016), and, most recently, Israel (2018).

This model has, nonetheless, attracted much criticism. For example, Kingston and Thomas (2019) argued that a coherent Nordic model is questionable, not least because Nordic laws operate in different contexts and are not implemented by practitioners or in existing legislation in the same way. Policy and law have thus become a mechanism for the transference of ideology and rhetoric. Other critics have focused on the risks the Nordic model could pose to sex workers' safety by increasing resources for policing their activities (Brooks-Gordon, 2006; Kingston & Thomas, 2019; Smith & Mac, 2018). Sex workers are invisible in this anti-prostitution crusade (McGarry & FitzGerald, 2018; Weitzer, 2007) precisely because their accounts clash with neo-abolitionist goals.

The international migration of the Nordic model (Kingston & Thomas, 2019; Pitcher, 2015, 2019; Vuolajärvi, 2019), the significant shift toward criminalization as the preferred strategy for governing commercial sex, and the use of punitive law enforcement to achieve this (Hammond, 2015; Sanders & Campbell, 2014) have all impacted the political regulation of the Israeli sex industry. On December 31, 2018, the Knesset (Israel's parliament) passed the Prohibition of Consumption of Prostitution Services Law – a watered-down version of the Nordic model which includes administrative fines with a voluntary alternative of participating in a preventive training course to replace a possible criminal record. The dramatic change in Israel's policy on sex commerce is the outcome of international pressure and an enduring local struggle led by state actors, NGOs, and journalists against the country's booming sex industry that began during the late 1990s and early 2000s.

Efforts to change Israel's sex work policy began in the early 2000s when local human rights and women's organizations lobbied the government to crack down on sex trafficking. Since their entreaties were brushed aside, they decided to take their campaign global and brought the issue before the United Nations and a US Congressional Committee. Due to political lobbying by Israeli parliament members, pressure by the US State Department, and the backing of international anti-trafficking organizations, what started as a prohibition on the sex trafficking of migrant women, mainly from the FSU (Former Soviet Union), and tracking of global sex trafficking organizations soon extended to include local sex industry regulations.

Almog (2016) explained that Israel, like many other countries, dealt with two main conflicting ideas: the sex work narrative and the prostitution-as-harm narrative. Until 2011, Israeli law supported a softened version of the sex work narrative. The sex industry existed in a legal gray area: while pimping, owning a brothel, and advertising were illegal, buying sex and being a sex worker were legal. However, the aforementioned international and local efforts and the definition of Israel as a Jewish and democratic state created an intersection between universal values of gender equality and Jewish values of protecting women's modesty and preserving family purity. The success of the End Demand policy in Israel resulted from determined efforts led by radical, neo-abolitionist, and conservative religious parliamentarians, who asserted that the unrestricted presence of sexual commerce abuses human rights, harms all women, and contradicts Jewish values (Lahav-Raz, 2020b; Levy-Aronovic et al., 2021).

Since 2011, neo-abolitionist governance has characterized various laws supporting the prostitution-as-harm narrative, which have earned overwhelming support in the Knesset from both the coalition government and the opposition. These laws include a ban on recruitment advertisements for prostitution (2017), a ban on strip clubs (2018), which defines lap dancing as an act of prostitution, and a ban on telephone lines used to advertise prostitution services (2018). In addition, two amendments to existing laws have been added: the first raised the punishment threshold for buying sex from a minor from three to five years; the second added prostitution to the list of offensive websites with restricted access (previously defined as websites dealing with gambling and incitement). The capstone of these legislative efforts was the Prohibition of Consumption of Prostitution Services Law, passed on December 31, 2018, and enacted on July 10, 2020. These various laws and amendments aim to eradicate different aspects of the sex industry, according to what has been called "morality politics" (Harrington, 2018; Pitcher, 2019; Weitzer, 2020).

Regardless of the immense efforts to eradicate the Israeli sex industry over the last two decades, it is interesting to see that, until 2016, there was no statistical data concerning the scope of Israel's sex industry and the characteristics of its main actors. Despite the consensus among government committees since the end of the 1990s regarding the need for statistical data to understand the sex industry phenomena, it was only in 2008 that the National Survey on the Phenomenon of Prostitution was launched. The survey was initiated by the Knesset Subcommittee on Combating Trafficking in Women and Prostitution and funded by the Ministry of Welfare and Social Services in cooperation with the Ministry of Internal Security. It was published eight years later, in 2016 (Santo et al., 2016), and indicated that over 12,500 people were involved in the sex industry, 95% of whom were cisgender women.

The survey examined aspects such as sex workers' motivations for entering the sex industry and demographic characteristics (e.g., age, origin, gender, family status, education, socioeconomic level, etc.). It also examined public attitudes toward sex work and financial aspects, revealing that the cumulative total of payments for sex work services in 2014 was 1.3 billion NIS (New Shekels). The findings of this survey have proved controversial with both legislators and sex workers, who argued that the statistics are dubious and are used to uphold a particular ideological viewpoint. Despite focusing on various aspects of the Israeli sex industry, the survey lacks substantive information on consumer patterns. The only data regarding consumption patterns referred to an estimated average of around five clients per day for each sex worker in discreet apartments or escort services and an estimated average of six clients per day for each sex worker in massage parlors. Moreover, the survey's findings indicated that, while being the smallest of all sex work scenes in Israel, street-based sex work comprises the highest number of consumers of all the sectors examined in the survey, with an average of almost seven clients on a workday. No attempt was made, however, to understand the characteristics and motivations of sex consumers.

Subsequently, researchers saw a need to fill this knowledge gap and learn more about sex consumers. For example, Shilo et al. (2021) explored the associations between views of men who pay for sex, their sociodemographic characteristics, and the frequency of their consumption. In a survey of 632 predominantly Jewish Israeli men aged 18–75, 32.3% stated having paid for sex more than once, and 11.1% stated having done so only once in their lifetime. Of the former, 51.1% reported paying for sex once every few years, 39.2% several times a year, and 9.7% several times a month or more. Other surveys based on representative samples of approximately 1000 Israeli men found that 20–30% of Israeli men have paid for sex at least once (Shilo & Mor, 2020; Shilo et al., 2020), and 16% have paid for sex on multiple occasions (Shilo et al., 2020). While respondents who reported having paid for sex were found to identify as non-religious, no other differences were found between them and those who have not paid for sex in terms of age, income, education levels, marital status, or number of children.

The Empirical Study

The sociological and cultural questions that inspired this book stem from the understanding that sex consumers' sexual reports are stories that serve as pathways for understanding both culture and the individuals operating in it. In this book, I use the "sociology of stories" (Berger & Quinney, 2004; Nuran, 2015; Plummer, 2002; Sanders, 2013) to address the sexual reports as stories that represent authentic knowledge formulated and uniquely expressed by the individual sex consumer. According to Showalter (1981), when analyzing stories, a researcher should use a "cultural reading" to uncover the different layers of the story, which contain both the expected hegemonic voice and the sometimes suppressed and silenced voice. Although Showalter was referring to women's voices, the same is true of men's voices, especially when operating in the context of the moral taint and stigma that characterizes sexual commerce. I, therefore, refer to sex consumers' online reports as stories reflecting what Grenz (2005) called "a self-discovery journey" in which the writer tells the story not only for their readers but, perhaps first of all, for themselves. The story may thus be informative for other readers, but it serves as a cure for its narrator, who is looking for relief, validation, redemption, and a desire for confession and liberation in front of their peers.

A cultural reading of the text also implies that every story expresses the writer's voice embedded in their cultural, national, and religious beliefs as well as ideological views. Sex consumers' stories, therefore, play an important role in perfecting the individuals' ability to articulate various cultural repertoires stemming from universal and local perceptions of sexuality and gender power relations. Furthermore, since technology and consumerism are inextricably intertwined (Illouz, 2007) and, as previously mentioned, sex consumption served for years as a "sexual closet," sex consumers rewrite sex consumption online as a moral, biological, social, and cultural system of shared beliefs and traditions. In return, these shared beliefs create a communal moral ethos that influences all actors operating in the sex industry. In other words, the collective imagination created in the online community by the collection of sexual stories not only remains in the individual consciousness but changes the reality of the Israeli sex industry.

The Aims of the Book

This book has two main objectives. The first is to offer an in-depth exploration of how various repertoires of masculinity characterize Israeli sex consumers operating online. The second is to explore the role of digital technology, combined with other spatial changes, in redrawing the rearrangement of modern-day sexual consumption. To achieve these objectives, the research questions are divided into three levels:

- *The content of the story*: what are sex consumers writing about? What is the meaning of the story written in the online community for the narrator himself and the community as a whole? Which masculine repertoires and components are reflected in their writing, and how do they organize their sexual experiences?
- *The relationship forged between community members*: what characterizes the community and the relationship between its members? What are the online community's values, norms, and rules, and how do they rearrange the meaning of a sexual report?
- *Digital spatial changes*: how do sex consumers use digital technology? How do they harness it for their needs and, in so doing, rearticulate and reformulate their relationship with sex workers? How does digital technology affect the intertwining of online and offline sex spaces?

Although the online forums declare themselves to be consumer forums, the community developed under the portal has long gone beyond its narrow role as a consumer community; rather, it is a community of the type that Bergs (2006) calls a "community of practice," in which members share common beliefs, values, forms of discourse, and the development of a common language. Looking to move beyond the narrow definition of a consumer community and follow the richness of the discourse, I conducted a discourse-centered online ethnography (Androutsopoulos & Beißwenger, 2008) in different time periods and on various digital platforms. The analysis of the sexual stories combined a variety of linguistic traditions to examine how individuals use discursive resources to establish relationships and interactions and how they construct their identity through digital platforms. The analysis included micro-linguistic and macro-discursive levels of observations of how discursive strategies contribute to creating community identity (Stommel, 2008).

Using a grounded theory approach (Strauss & Corbin, 1994), the goal here was not to argue for or against the "truth" of specific statements in the text. Rather, I attempted to understand people's life experiences in the most rigorous and detailed way while identifying categories emerging from the text and then locating them within a historical and social context (Caldas-Coulthard, 1993). In this sense, the text offers a window into a person's life experience (Charmaz, 2000; Ryan & Bernard, 2000), also examining the role of language (Agar, 1994; Spender, 1980) in creating a particular reality and the social relationships and ideologies promoted through speech.

The Data Sources

The data in this book was gathered in three online ethnographic studies over three different time periods and using various Israel-based digital platforms. The main source was an online ethnography conducted between 2012 and 2015 on nine forums that were part of an Israeli internet sex portal founded in 2007. The portal offers various sex services, including an extensive array of 28 client review forums where individuals can discuss many issues. Of the 28 forums, 24 were open and could be read by anyone, but registration with a username and password was necessary to write a review. Following Weitzer's (2000) claim that indoor and outdoor sex work venues attract different clientele, the data was taken from forums representing both.

Due to the understanding that different sexual arenas can produce different discourses of masculinity, the second data source was taken from an online ethnography conducted between 2017 and 2018 on an online forum for Israeli sex tourists. This forum was part of the same online sex portal and thus enabled further examination of the online community's development.

Since the Prohibition of Consumption of Prostitution Law was legislated in 2018 and came into force in 2020, during the first two periods of data collection, the practice of paying or being paid for sex in Israel was legal for adults, except for soliciting to which the police tended to look the other way (Amir & Amir, 2004). Nonetheless, the active efforts by feminist organizations to attach shame and stigma to the sex industry over the last two decades and the subsequent widespread social labeling have intensified the general tendency of sex consumers to stress the normative nature of their actions. Furthermore, in a recent survey, 20% of Israeli men who regularly pay for sex stated they would cease consuming sex in Israel once the law takes effect and would, instead, pursue their activities abroad (Shilo et al., 2020). This indicates the centrality of the Israeli public discourse portraying sex consumers as abusive and deviant in shaping the experiences of Israeli sex consumers both in Israel and abroad.

As part of the End Demand legislation in 2017, the Knesset added prostitution to the list of offensive websites with restricted access. This dramatically affected the regulation of the Israeli sex industry and Israeli sex consumers.

The State Attorney's Office demanded the closure of the online sex portal I was using as a data source on the grounds that it violated the law prohibiting the publication of prostitution ads. Although not the only Israeli sex portal, it was the largest and most prominent and drew much public attention. While, to date, the sex portal still exists, the legal battles, the accompanying public attention, and its repeated closures caused sex consumers to migrate to other digital platforms. Therefore, the third data source for this book was an online ethnography conducted between 2021 and 2022 on Telegram, which is today the most popular and active arena for Israeli sex consumers. Founded in 2013, Telegram is a globally accessible freemium online messaging app. It provides optional, end-to-end encrypted chats, video calling, VoIP, and file sharing. Since Telegram prioritizes security and speed and offers deletable secret chats, it has become the preferred channel for Israeli sex consumers. Data was gathered from four main Telegram channels: "Forum Abroad," "Main Forum," "Sugar Daddy Forum," and the "Trash Talk Forum." All the quotes in the book were originally written in Hebrew and were translated by the author. An effort has been made to remain as faithful as possible to the original meaning of the text.

Concerning the authenticity and reliability of the information, there is rich discussion in the literature regarding the quality of the knowledge produced when the space allows the anonymity of the user and, consequently, its degree of reliability. Indeed, Earle and Sharp (2016) claimed that online arenas might contribute to the "filterization" of one's identity. Nonetheless, anonymity can also allow for presenting a more authentic identity by releasing inhibitions. According to Suler (2004), the online release of inhibitions works in two opposite directions: "benign disinhibition," which enables users to express hidden feelings, fears, and intimacy, and "toxic disinhibition," which is expressed in rude language, anger, and hatred. Users' online identity, which contains both of these aspects, is no less authentic than their offline identity. If such exists, the invented elements are part of the "real" identity, namely, part of the individual's personality.

Accordingly, although it is possible for a sex consumer to glorify himself and his sexual performance or to describe a fabricated reality, this does not invalidate the truth of the act for the person writing his report on the forum; it just shifts the focus of interest from the question of the reality of the events to the writer's choice to include them in his written sexual report. These stories are therefore treated throughout this book as narratives reflecting various truths embedded in the individual's identity.

Ethical Considerations

The research presented in this book is purely observational, thus opening it up to the claim that the researcher is a "specialized type of lurker" (Di Guardo & Castriotta, 2014, p. 83). However, as Berdychevsky and Nimrod (2017) noted, such studies provide vibrant and authentic data while avoiding the difficulties in directly questioning sensitive issues.

In fact, this book challenges the perspective that the "lurker" gives the researcher greater power; instead, it reflects how participants sometimes stay in the dark while the researcher becomes visible. This was specifically illustrated in a discussion in the Central Lobby forum of the online portal on June 29, 2015, which wanted to draw members' attention to a Facebook page called "When He Pays," which uploads quotes from the various sex portal forums. In an ensuing discussion among the members, one member wrote that he knew of a doctoral student researching the community. (I could only assume that he had been present at one of my lectures on the subject or read texts I wrote and published). It became clear from the various responses that most community members are aware of the forum's publicity but are not bothered by the presence of "lurkers" such as journalists, activists, and researchers, perceiving them as an integral part of the field.

Nevertheless, as Sanders et al. (2017) expressed, studying the online performances of sex industry clients brings ethical, methodological, and epistemological complications into this form of research. Consequently, the growing body of research on online communities of sex industry clients (Blevins & Holt, 2009; Holt & Blevins, 2007; Horswill & Weitzer, 2018; Huff, 2011; Tyler & Jovanovski, 2018) has defined the ethical issues relating to consent, permission, and privacy. Accordingly, no user consent is required for the research when a site describes itself as open and public. In addition, the ethical issue regarding the researcher's power must be addressed by choosing, analyzing, and interpreting the texts.

Even though all the platforms used for this research are public and open for reading, all nicknames (themselves anonymous) and any other identifying details of the digital platform and the writers were erased to protect participants' anonymity and maintain confidentiality. As Tyler and Jovanovski (2018) claimed, online reviews should not be read as objective accounts but rather as a particular version of events with other consumers as the intended audience. This book's approach to the language of Israeli sex industry consumers, therefore, embraces a plurality of meanings, and my analysis is just one of many possible data readings.

2   The Consumer Sexual Script

> There are members here who ate a lot of shit and put their necks on the line[1] to report so that the rest would take things into account and learn lessons for better or for worse.
>
> (Central Lobby Forum,
> November 4, 2015).

> I don't get it! There are 1800 views and only four comments! Just that is proof of all the free riders.[2] Instead of sharing, people just read my posts, but they don't replay and share their thoughts and experiences. No one is willing to put themselves out there for others. Instead of complaining all the time, take out your wallet and give something back to the community.
>
> (Discreet Apartments Forum,
> February 14, 2014)

"Putting your neck on the line" and "free rider" have become two of the most common expressions used by Israeli sex consumers when sharing their written sexual experiences with each other. What can be learned about the Israeli sex consumer community from the fact that, when describing their sexual experiences, members choose to represent the community and the feelings and emotions of its members by using these two slang expressions? Following an understanding that these are key concepts in the creation of the Israeli sex consumers community, this chapter examines the origin and meanings of these expressions among Israeli sex consumers and how they reflect the way community members adopt, understand, and implement the ideals of consumer culture in their sex-buying experiences.

While the Israeli sex consumer community aims to share instrumental information with its members, a deep analysis offers a glimpse of one of the central cultural motifs of Israeli society that is tied tightly to heteronormative masculinity in Israel. I argue that the two concepts of "putting your neck on the line" and "free rider" are two sides of the same coin: the constant moral boundary work aimed at avoiding being a *freier*. The first expression, "putting your neck on the line," refers to a person who sacrifices themself for the sake of others

DOI: 10.4324/9781003128670-2

and thus asks for the individual's ongoing sacrifice on behalf of the collective. The second expression, "free rider," refers to a person who takes advantage of a situation to live at the expense of others. It thus warns the individual against parasitic behavior that may turn them and others into *freiers*, namely, individuals who have been exploited and cheated by others. The consumer sexual script, therefore, becomes an interesting interpretive lens for examining the implementation of consumer culture with local cultural characteristics while exploring what Roniger and Feige (1992) described as the coexistence of individualism and collectivism that characterizes Israeli society.

Following a short description of consumerism within Israeli culture, the chapter goes on to show how the centrality of the *freier*/anti-*freier* model impacts the consumer sexual script of Israeli sex consumers.

Consumerism Within Israeli Culture, or Why Are Israelis So Afraid of Being *Freiers*?

Various scholars (Brents & Hausbeck, 2007; Frank, 2003a) have argued that the way the sex industry is organized and sex is marketed as a product is the outcome of the interweaving of economy and culture. Accordingly, current sexual consumption patterns cannot be understood without turning the gaze on the culture itself. Viewing consumerism as a sexual script allows us to discern sex work encounters as complex economic transactions mediated by various cultural practices. In the Israeli case, universal consumer rationality is combined with a unique feature of Israeli society: the anti-*freier* model. The fear of being a *freier*, an idiom with an imposing meaning, has become a central symbolic model and a metonym for Israeli culture.

According to Roniger and Feige (1992, 1993), who were the first to trace the sociological evolution of the *freier* phenomenon, the word *freier* is originally from German (derived from *frei* [free] and *herr* [man]) and then spread into Polish and Yiddish and later into both Hebrew and Russian. The dominant meaning in German referred to a man of high social standing who was free from certain constraints and a man courting a woman. In modern German, it is used to denote clients of prostitutes. Its linguistic absorption in Israel, however, entailed an inversion of meanings that expresses a multivocality shaped through local social processes but is mainly crowded out by a cluster of connotations focused on naivety. Roniger and Feige (1992, 1993) argued that while *freier* shares with the English word sucker the meaning of finishing on the losing end of an exchange in an individualistic and capitalistic context, in the case of Israel, it has an additional meaning of acting out of context in a collectivistic manner. Hence, a *freier* denotes a naive person willing to contribute to cooperative endeavors while others may choose instead to free ride. The image of a *freier* is therefore an individual who is doomed to be cheated and exploited by others' shrewdness and willingness to take advantage of their efforts toward maintaining cooperation and the common good.

Roniger and Feige (1993) focused mainly on how the anti-*freier* model reflects the dialectical tension between collectivism and individualism in Israeli society in which neither individualistic pragmatism nor collectivistic engagements entirely obscure each other. For them, it symbolizes the progressive decline of collectivistic ideology as depicted in the image of the Halutz – an individual who, unselfishly and often through hardship, contributes voluntarily to the collective well-being without a clear notion of compensation. The decline of the Halutz and the rise of the anti-*freier* as a key symbol reflect a transformation in the connection between individuals and their community – a central issue for Israeli society which is grounded in a communitarian ideology. Hence, Roniger and Feige (1993) explained the anti-*freier* becomes a powerful mode of resistance to the hegemonic national ideology and mirrors the social process of the unwillingness of individuals to contribute personal resources to their community with no guarantee of substantial return. While Israeli society adopted and embraced an individualistic ideology, it still maintains collective goals and continues to make huge demands on its citizens, such as mandatory military service and high taxes. Consequently, collectivist and individualistic ideologies coexist, and the *freier* and anti-*freier* models, which derive from their dialectical relations with mainstream Zionist ideology, reflect this paradoxical existence.

Later sociological and anthropological observations on the *freier* phenomenon (Bloch, 1998, 2003; Bloch & Lemish, 2005; Yair, 2011) referred to its centrality in Israeli society and showed its manifestation in all levels of communication and among all echelons of society, age groups, and ethnic origins in all frameworks. Others showed its salience on various media platforms (Cohen-Shalev, 2019; Telmon, 2001) and in the Israeli culinary scene (Avieli, 2018). The *freier* phenomenon is such a central part of Israeli culture that to be a *freier* is regularly touted as the absolute antithesis of what Israelis aspire to be. Yair (2011) even claimed that Israelis are tormented by one main anxiety: not to be perceived as *freiers*, which can, for many, be experienced as social death or a loss of one's humanity. The cultural code against being a *freier* motivates Israelis to conduct a never-ending war against the possibility of humiliation; if you manage to make someone else a *freier* and prove yourself an anti-*freier*, you have triumphed in the Israeli zero-sum game: the struggle for survival.

The *freier* is common in various areas of social life but, most frequently, in reference to financial transactions. Bloch (2003) showed that *freier* behavior in market exchanges results from non-competitive pricing, being cheated, or not getting what one paid for. Hence, in financial terms, to be a *freier* entails coming out of a transaction at a disadvantage – as a loser. Yair (2011) added that the fear of being a *freier* directs all consumer choices made by Israelis. Israeli consumers, therefore, try to obtain all the information that others have before buying and thus ensure they pay no more than them. The aim here is not consumer efficiency but rather the guarantee of not being humiliated in the eyes of one's acquaintances. The fear of being shown a *freier* with its poten-tial humiliation becomes Israeli consumers' main consumption motivation. Paradoxically, this results in a consumption characteristic defined by "herd behavior," according to which individuals collaborate as part of a group, often making decisions they would not make individually. Moreover, the cultural code of the anti-*freier* leads to exploitative patterns: the goal is to reach the target, and there is no taboo regarding the means. The main principle is not to follow the rules because whoever obeys the rules is a *freier* (Yair, 2011), thus reflecting Roniger and Feige's (1993) argument that the anti-*freier* model demonstrates the dialectical coexistence of collectivism and individualism.

While scholars (e.g., Aviely, 2017; Yair, 2011) have shown the relevance of the *freier* model to all echelons of society, there is agreement that the values espoused by those aspiring not to be *freiers* are more compatible with mas-culine than feminine culture (Roniger & Feige, 1993). According to Bloch (2003), the anti-*freier* model is most readily detected in the male-dominated public sphere: financial transactions, the political arena, military service, and car-driving behaviors. Bloch and Lemish (2005) went on to show that being a *freier* is frequently equated with a lack of the type of masculinity that rests on power displays, confrontation, competition, and a total disregard for the other. Since coming out as a *freier* entails playing a zero-sum game in which you either win or lose, it is deemed more typical of masculinity. From this understanding of the centrality of the *freier* and anti-*freier* model in Israeli consumption patterns and its prevalence among heteronormative masculinity, I now go on to show how the consumer sexual script of Israeli sex consumers is characterized by the attempt to avoid being a *freier*. This attempt is con-ducted in front of two different but complementary social actors – sex workers and community members – and entails avoiding being a *freier* in front of the former and turning the latter into *freiers*.

The Struggle Against Being a *Freier* in Front of Sex Workers

Prior and Peled's (2021) meta-synthesis of sex consumers' identity construc-tion revealed the immanence of consumerism discourse among sex consum-ers. They found that sex consumers described paying for sex as normative consumer behavior, which reinforced their "successful" masculine consum-erist identity. Their findings conform with others (Hammond & Van Hooff, 2020; Shumka et al., 2017) who claimed that the power of neoliberal consum-erist discourse is closely tied with hegemonic masculinity and is a sign of the successful masculine consumerist identity of men who can buy whatever they desire. Sex consumers, therefore, draw on their economic resources and use the market to find sexual fulfillment while also addressing issues of sexual dissatisfaction. In so doing, they frame buying sexual services from women as a normative masculine act.

The intersections of consumerism and masculinity have turned sex-purchasing venues into heteronormative spaces (Colosi, 2020) in which consumers, albeit in different ways, use masculinizing practices to perform heteronormative masculinity (Connell, 1996, 2005). An analysis of the Israeli sex consumer community reveals that their masculinizing practices involve internalizing a market ideology of neoliberal rationalization combined with the Israeli fear of becoming *freiers*. Becoming a *freier*, in this case, means being emasculated by sex workers, which consumers constantly perceive as a threat of exploitation and humiliation. For example, in an online forum for Israeli sex tourists, one member wrote:

> Bro, the girls in Odessa, are not *freiers*. It shows that they see you as "ATMs." Don't spread money for nothing, and don't fall in love with any-one there. No one there will be your friend, it's a business, and they are saleswomen – it's harsh but true.
>
> (March 14, 2017)

The neoliberal market rationalization, which impacts how we think about sexual transactions, is not unique to Israeli sex consumers. In recent years, there has been growing research attention to consumerist identity construc-tion within the context of online forums for sex consumers (Lahav-Raz, 2019; Pettinger, 2011, 2015; Tyler & Jovanovski, 2018). These studies have high-lighted sex consumers' self-portrayal as disappointed and deprived customers who are powerless to complain about the bad service received in paid sex encounters. They have also shown how sex consumers seek to maximize their gain at the expense of the perceived exploitative corporations that have taken advantage of them and rendered them powerless consumers.

However, among Israeli sex consumers, commonsense market rationality becomes a struggle for survival. Still, since it is a zero-sum game, you are either a *freier*, i.e., you were used by someone else, or you are not a *freier*, because you made someone else a *freier*. Being on the losing end also means losing your mas-culine self, and Israeli sex consumers are thus preoccupied with constant bound-ary work (Lamont, 2012) in an attempt to predict who will try and take advantage of them. When the writer of the above post states that "the girls in Odessa are not *freiers*," he means that they will not let themselves be exploited by others; indeed, as mentioned earlier, the *freier*/anti-*freier* model can also refer to femi-nine behavior. However, in this zero-sum game, if sex workers are not *freiers*, the danger of being humiliated by them becomes a constant struggle for existence: either you exploit or you are exploited. This is reflected in the following posts:

> There was also some hot 21-year-old Russian girl I sat down to talk with, and after a few seconds, she told me that if I wanted us to continue talking, I had to pay her! Good luck, sweetie. Find yourself another *freier* from all the jackasses around here. Not me!
>
> (Sex Tourists Forum, September 7, 2017)

All the girls who ask for high amounts without sharing their photos don't do it because they are something special but because they are looking for the "*freier* of the day."

(Telegram, Sugar Daddy Forum, February 18, 2021)

These examples reflect Bloch's (2003) assertion that the *freier* model evaluates every situation according to the threat it might pose to a person's reputation. Regarding sex consumption, Israeli sex consumers use this model to assess the threat posed by sex workers and reflect on how Israeli culture turns them into *freiers*. Discussions about what makes one a *freier* in consumption terms are especially prevalent among Israeli men who consume sex abroad. The transition between countries allows for a comparative reflection on the consumer norms in different places and their translation from one culture to another. For many, their sexual experiences abroad strengthen the feeling that they are treated as *freiers* in Israel:

I will write a detailed report on my sexual experiences in Germany. Still, one thing stood out… how much we Israelis are *freiers* in Israel and how there is no connection in Israel between what you pay and the appearance and quality of the girl you get.

(Sex Tourists Forum, September 26, 2017)

Today, Israeli women are part of the system and come ready to sting us. When you fly abroad three times in six months, you understand what is happening here and that we are all *freiers*.

(Telegram, Sugar Daddy Forum, November 8, 2021)

Hence, for Israeli sex consumers, the constant struggle for existence, according to which being a *freier* constitutes social death (Yair, 2011), dictates consumer choices both in Israel and abroad. Furthermore, sexual experiences abroad are organized through the attempt to avoid being a *freier* and also indicate Israeli consumers' ongoing frustration that consuming sex in Israel involves constant humiliation at the hands of sex workers.

One of the common themes over the years in all the platforms examined is sex consumers' perception that Israeli sex workers use their life stories to exploit them and turn them into *freiers*. For example, in the Sugar Daddy Forum on Telegram, there was an argument about the price increase in the sex industry and how it reflects sex workers' consumer power and leaves sex consumers powerless. One member wrote that consumers need to understand that sex work is not like any other job and that consumers should treat sex workers with respect and sensitivity due to their life histories. Another member responded:

Because of this attitude, the situation today in terms of service in Israel is the way it is. Continue to defend them and then write that you behaved well and she pissed on you. If she doesn't want to sleep with men, she should go and work somewhere else and not be a sex worker. As if someone is forcing her. As if there are no women who work as waitresses or in the kitchen. Why do you think that in our work, we don't take shit from the customers but still provide service because it's our livelihood? But I forgot that a woman is a sacred creature who needs mercy. *Freiers*!

(Telegram, Sugar Daddy Forum, May 8, 2022).

This member's response challenges studies showing that consumers try to forge "romantic intimacy" and that their engagement with the sex industry involves emotional and intimate needs (Bernstein, 2007; Colosi, 2020; Hammond & Van Hooff, 2020; Milrod & Weitzer, 2012; Sanders, 2008, 2013). It also indicates the perception of the *freier* as a consumer who does not understand the nature of economic transactions. The *freier*'s attempts to obscure financial relationships through the illusion of emotional ones means that he has failed to present a successful masculine consumerist identity. As the argument between the members continued, one member accused another of harming sex workers' livelihood when he tried to lower their prices. The latter replied:

You are harmful to Israel on all levels. You have no problem lying and twisting things. I am no *freier* that you can put words in my mouth. For example, where did I write that I would set a price on the woman's body? I claim they say one thing, but then they get their money, finish you off, and lie to you. It's called twisting someone around your little finger. But you don't have an answer to that, so you twist things with your left-wing feminist claims "to treat her like a human being, not an object." Once again, those mantras! We treat them too nicely, and they give us the opposite. Enough! Defend the men who eat shit from women for once.

(Telegram, Sugar Daddy Forum, May 8, 2022).

At the beginning of the 1990s, Roniger and Feige (1993) described the increasingly widespread use of the *freier* concept in public discourse as reflecting operative changes in the perceptions of Israeli society and its members' subjectivities. They argued that the term *freier*'s expanded meaning reflected the political leadership's growing loss of credibility and growing public cynicism in the 1970s as society distanced itself from the once overwhelming grip of the hegemonic discourse of the Halutz, which was still largely endorsed by the state. This public cynicism led to the political turnover of 1977 that ended over 40 years of the Labor Party's political hegemony in Israel. The rise of the anti-*freier* model thus became a modus vivendi and a symbol of resistance to the left-wing ideology characterized by the Labor Party.

The previous post demonstrates the evolution of the *freier* model in Israel since the period Roniger and Feige (1993) were writing about. It contains not only the perception of the *freier* as a gullible, naive, and innocent consumer who can be easily exploited but also the *freier*'s assumed association with those who hold left-wing and feminist views. This association can be explained as a result of two social processes Israel has undergone in recent years: the first concerns the delegitimization of left-wing ideology, and the second concerns recent changes in Israeli policy toward the sex industry.

Regarding the delegitimization of left-wing ideology, scholars have shown that the prevailing febrile atmosphere in Israel entails incitement against the small and ever-dwindling number of Israeli Jews on the political left, who are now frequently denounced as "traitors" and "radical anti-Zionists" (Abd Abad & Hiev, 2019; Mandelbaum, 2012; Waxman, 2016) It has, consequently, become an insult to be called a leftist in Israel today, and those who publicly identify themselves as such run the risk of social stigma and even physical threats. The Israeli left was and still is identified with the key symbol of the Halutz and, therefore, with the Ashkenazi hegemony. As such, in the current political climate, there is a tendency to see leftists not only as *freiers*, i.e., those who still believe in outdated ideals and mistaken dreams (such as peace with the Palestinians), but also as traitors. This is reflected in the words of the previous quote: "You are harmful to Israel on all levels."

Mandelbaum (2012) showed how attempts to redefine the semantic field of the "left" by delegitimatizing organizations that work for a better and equal society are bound by placing them within a semantic field predicated as "radical," which excludes their role and opinion in society. The metonym of the left with a radical view is also closely related to feminist struggles that have taken place in the last decades in Israel, including the extensive feminist struggle against the country's booming sex industry that began during the late 1990s and early 2000s. As a result, in the past decade, the view that paying for sex is a form of violence against women has increasingly gained currency in the Israeli public, professional, and social advocacy discourses (Lahav-Raz, 2020b; Levy-Aronovic et al., 2021; Prior & Peled, 2019). This was evident in a public campaign to criminalize the purchasing of sex, which culminated on December 31, 2018, when the Knesset passed the Prohibition of Consumption of Prostitution Law. Israel became the eighth country in the world to join the controversial regulatory experiment of incriminating consumers of the sex industry.

The implementation of an End Demand policy in Israel resulted from the collaboration between feminist MKs from both ends of the political and ideological map: right-wing national-religious and ultra-orthodox Jewish feminists on the one hand and left-wing secular radical feminists on the other. However, in Israeli public discourse, especially among sex consumers who endure the stigma of their actions, this struggle is still identified as the outcome of the efforts of radical leftist feminists. Hence, understanding the sociopolitical processes that Israeli society has undergone in recent decades shows how the image of the contemporary *freier* involves not only naivety but also leftism and even, to a large extent, a complete renunciation of femininity. Thus, the *freier*, which served for years as an antithetical model to what Israelis have aspired to be, mirrors contemporary Israeli culture. For sex consumers, being a *freier* means not only experiencing humiliation at the hands of sex workers within a market relationship but becoming a danger to one's masculine self.

Those who behave like *freiers* risk, in addition, the humiliation of being accused of holding left-wing, radical, feminist ideologies, i.e., being emasculated, and the shaming of the entire male community. This points to the delicate boundary work required by community members and shows how the *freier* entwines within it the dialectical coexistence of individualism and collectivism that characterizes Israeli society.

The Struggle to Prevent Turning Others in the Community into *Freiers*

As previously argued, the *freier* model dictates Israeli sex consumer choices in front of sex workers and, mainly, within the male community participating in the sexual recreation. The importance given to homosociality can be explained by what scholars (Colosi, 2020; Frank, 2003b; Grazian, 2007; Liepe-Levinson, 2003) have shown regarding the need of sex consumers to present their normative masculine identity to one another and, in doing so, gain mutual acceptance and respect. This reflects the importance of homosociality and the need for group acknowledgment of the correct performance of normative masculinity and supports consumers' identities as heterosexual males, providing them with confidence in their masculinity and heterosexual power performance.

Following, I demonstrate how Israeli sex consumers' online communities have become what Kaplan and Haenlien (2010) called "collaborative projects." This means that many actors' joint efforts lead to a better outcome for themselves than one actor could achieve individually. These online communities, created initially on the online sex portal and then migrating to Telegram, have long evolved from the narrow scope of sharing instrumental details about sexual experiences and ranking sex workers' performances. It has transformed its members into what I described elsewhere (Lahav-Raz, 2019) as sex prosumers who both produce and consume simultaneously. The concept of the prosumer is based on the sociology of consumption and is a term associated with Toffler (1980) that refers to the combination of a producer and a consumer. However, the concept developed new meanings as the shift toward Web 2.0 altered digital environments, causing productive paradigms to be reshuffled in favor of prosumers.

The prosumer concept is highly relevant for understanding current sexual purchasing patterns, mainly since most sex commerce is mediated online. As Ritzer and Jurgenson (2010) argued, the prosumer concept has become a defining feature of online consumption practices since the internet thrust us into a new age of capitalism labeled "prosumer capitalism." This may explain the development of the Israeli community as a collective prosumerism aligned with Paltrinieri and Esposti's (2013) digital prosumerism characteristics, according to which each individual is required to contribute content to the community for the benefit of all.

For Israeli sex consumers, beyond the narrow scope of "improving service conditions and ensuring a good sexual experience,"[3] this collaborative project aims to ensure that community members will not turn each other into *freiers*. Regarding the Israeli *freier*, Bloch (2003) showed that for the person choosing to be or not to be a *freier*, the important thing is what other actors will think of their behavior; the appreciation of the peer group is, therefore, all-important. The *freier* model means that Israeli sex consumer online discussions are often diverted from the sexual experiences themselves to the meaning of sharing in front of the entire community. As a result, a community ethic concerning the moral behavior expected of all its members develops. This turns sex consumption as collective prosumerism into not just the obvious step of market forces but also a moral response to what sex consumers view as an inversion which enables others – sex workers and community members alike – to exploit them, turning them into *freiers*.

To avoid turning others into *friers,* one of the sex portal admins published a post on November 11, 2015, titled: "A quick guide on how to write a useful report." He outlined six commandments which included emphasizing coordination accessibility and giving a description of the meeting place, identifying details of the sex worker, preferably with a link, as well as details of the sex worker's appearance and the sexual services she offers, and more. At the end of his post, alongside sharing several examples of successful reports from community members, he wrote:

> Not everyone was born with writing talent. This is not a creative writing competition. The goal is to share as many details as possible with your friends here. A report can also be negative since we don't enjoy every situation. However, even if you didn't enjoy it, we'll be happy to hear, so we don't fall. Give a reliable report – preserve your and our honor.

Connell and Messerschmidt claimed that hegemonic masculinity is the "most honored way of being a man, signaling men's dominance over women. While it's not embodied by most men, it is nonetheless a gendered ideal that maintains heteronormativity" (2005, p. 832). This post demonstrates the emphasis Israeli sex consumers place on collective masculine honor, which, in this case, is based on reliability and comradeship – characteristics associated with hegemonic masculinity. To achieve manly virtue, it is common among Israeli sex consumers to describe both successful sexual experiences and unpleasant experiences which involve disappointment, failure, and rejection. When a community member shares a bad sexual experience, he usually gets comforting responses encouraging and praising his sacrifice and dedication to the entire community. Following are a number of reactions illustrating the reactions of members of the community to a sexual report of an unsuccessful sexual experience that appeared in the Discreet Apartments Forum on October 13, 2012:

> This is what's known as putting your neck on the line.
>
> Thanks for putting your neck on the line.
>
> As usual, you have described things accurately, for better or for worse.
>
> At the end of the day, we are lucky to have someone like you in the forum willing to invest time and resources in doing and putting his neck on the line.
>
> You should feel good about yourself. I applaud your effort in reporting and putting your neck on the line.

Within the Israeli sex consumer community, "putting one's neck on the line" implies that sharing a poor sexual experience with the rest of the community is a sacrifice since the individual is willing to sacrifice his honor to expose his weaknesses and humiliation to his fellow consumers. He thus contributes to the community by warning others and helping prevent their similar embarrassment of "falling." The use of the phrase by Israeli sex consumers associates Connell's (2009) universal masculine ethic of self-sacrifice for the sake of others with what was perceived in the past as the organizing cultural code of Israeli society: individuals willing to sacrifice themselves for their community.

However, as Roniger and Feige (1993) pointed out, the anti-*freier* model means that Israelis are only inclined to "put their neck on the line" if others do the same. If others choose to free ride, this means that the individual has turned into a *freier*. Therefore, for Israeli sex consumers, consumerism is bound with individual and collective self-sacrifice. As such, the community encourages its members to contribute to the collective by "putting their neck on the line" for the protection of others by praising and glorifying the individual who did so and, at the same time, warning members against becoming "free riders":

> And one more thing about all the free riders. Not only do they not write reviews, but they also send me private messages asking for further details. Have you no shame?
>
> (Discreet Apartments Forum, October 25, 2012)

"Free riders" are community members who are seen to express parasitic behavior: they do not contribute to the community, but demand others do so by asking questions and using community resources, thus exploiting other members by not contributing to the collective. Many community members testified that a sense of exploitation emerges when the prevailing feeling is one of the utilitarian relationships between members and there is disregard of others' sacrifices:

> I'm stunned at how a member can read others' reports and ask them questions but doesn't respond by saying a good word or indicating whether he liked reading the description. Why ignore it so blatantly? You're already writing, so try a little harder. If we don't support each other, if we don't appreciate and know how to give back, then, eventually, people won't stay here even for "just a question."
>
> (Street Forum, August 30, 2012)

In the earlier discussion of the fear of appearing a *freier* in front of sex workers, the *freier* was seen to be the one who tries to establish an illusion of emotional relationships, i.e., he fails to understand the nature of the instrumental relationship between sex workers and clients. Here, however, in this post about the relationship between community members, we see the opposite taking place. When a community member enacts instrumentalizing behavior toward a fellow member, he fails to understand the emotional meaning of the community – the reciprocity and intimate sharing, homosociality, and brotherhood – which are all channeled exclusively for the sake of the community. In so doing, he turns all others into *freiers*.

Since Israeli consumerism is intertwined with anti-*freier* behavior, obtaining information before buying is necessary to avoid becoming a *freier*. When one chooses not to use community resources, one turns into a *freier*:

> Thank you, brother, for reporting even though you fell; but if you had searched the forum before going as far as that particular place, you would not have fallen like that.
>
> (Street Forum, May 22, 2013)

Beyond justifying the community's existence, this post demonstrates how the community provides a framework of collective consumerism which aims to protect members from becoming *freiers* or "falling." The emphasis on writing and sharing sexual experiences develops a community ethic according to which "putting one's neck on the line" for another member, which in other social arenas might be mercilessly mocked as *freier* behavior, enjoys a narrative of righteousness and community mission.

However, not all collective initiatives are welcomed and praised. In a discussion following a consumer's report of a price increase, one of the members of the Sugar Daddy Forum suggested that they should create a collective consumer protest since the current situation turns them into *freiers*. When others claimed this was impossible, he chose to attack them:

> You are the most *freier* nation in history. You think you're the smartest. That's why everything is expensive in Israel. From the supermarket to fuel, to apartments, and to hookers. You think you're the sugar daddies, but the truth is that you're the hookers. You're being fucked from all directions.
>
> (Telegram, Sugar Daddy Forum, August 2, 2022)

This again highlights the obsession in Israeli society with not being a *freier* and its association with proving one's masculinity. The *freier*/anti-*freier* model is used here by forum members as a verbal expression to define themselves and their relationships with other members, to situate their perceptions of the world around them, and to determine subsequent courses of action. The model also demonstrates the coexistence of individualistic and collectivist values. The *freier* is a cheated individual, but when individuals in society are unwilling to contribute to the collective, then the entire nation becomes a nation of *freiers*. Furthermore, the attempt to prevent others from becoming *freiers* causes a constant clash between members concerning who is the real *freier*. There is, therefore, frequent bickering between members who claim that one should be cautious of following the recommendations of certain members since this will turn others into *freiers*:

> Beware of his "recommendations." He doesn't really understand and will direct you to trashy places that suit Israeli *freiers*.
>
> (Sex Tourists Forum, May 20, 2018)

> I wouldn't suggest you get recommendations from someone stupid enough to pay a girl an extra 50 euros for a handjob without fucking. These Israeli *freiers* pay 600 for Ukraine's garbage and then fly to Germany and ruin all the good there. He is a scumbag who doesn't understand what he's talking about. His recommendations are suitable for *freiers* like him. According to your report, you are the only one who came out as a *freier*, and not for the first time.
>
> (Sex Tourists Forum, May 20, 2018)

The delicate boundary work required from community members in order not to be a *freier* or turn others into *freiers* is especially present among Israeli sex consumers abroad. What may be perceived as typical Israeli behavior there and praised as managing to avoid being a *freier* in Israel may risk tarnishing, humiliating, and staining the entire Israeli male community and even Israel itself:

There were very nice guys waiting in line. They were very polite people, and I also represented Israel with great honor. So, whoever goes there, be polite and try to be first in line without pushing in line like the average Israeli... If you are a disgusting person and cannot control yourself, please say you are Turkish or from some Arab country. Don't say you are Israeli. We have a good name there, God knows why.

(Sex Tourist Forum, September 13, 2017)

While standing in line may seem like a minor issue, it is a good example of the Israeli lack of trust in the state and its institutions. According to Karniel (2005), standing in line is integral to the social framework and expresses the public's confidence in the system before which it stands. Hence, standing in line reflects the belief that it is fair to provide service to the person who arrived first and acceptance of the value and principle of equality between the people standing in line. Standing in line also implies recognition of all the elements of trust: there is a purpose to standing in line because, in the end, I will get something I want or need. Similarly, it manifests partnership and trust in the values it reflects: equality, human dignity, and faith in the rule of law in the sense that those who do not stand in line or do not respect the line (by, for example, pushing in or going to the front) may be punished.

In the 1990s, Roniger and Feige (1993) claimed that the anti-*freier* symbolizes the individual's lack of trust in the leadership. In the absence of shared values, goals, and interests, it is impossible to have a society whose members stand in line. When Israelis go to receive a service, they do not trust the system, the service provider, or the surrounding public. Since they cannot assume that the basic values of the line will be preserved, they must cheat, overtake, or push others to get service. By standing in line, the individual fails to understand the internal cultural code and becomes a *freier*.

Understanding how such a minor issue as standing in line reflects the lack of trust among Israelis may clarify why the writer of the previous post prioritizes standing in line. It indicates the careful boundary work, according to which the most important thing for an Israeli is to be first in line since the lack of trust in the system – any system – is immanent. However, at the same time, it reflects the understanding that Israeli behavior, which would have earned the writer respect in Israel for not becoming a *freier*, may be condemned elsewhere. Furthermore, in a society that does not trust its individual members, it is no wonder that sex consumers see sex workers as part of the system, as was shown in an earlier post: "Today, Israeli women are part of the system and come ready to sting us." The inability to stand in line, as bound by the *freier* and anti-*freier* models, symbolizes the lack of a similar interpretation of collective values and the inherent mistrust among individuals. This has become the organizing principle of Israeli social life, namely, a zero-sum game of survival in which you are either a *freier* or an anti-*freier*.

To conclude, Tyler (2004) argued that the development of sexuality as governed according to neoliberal principles and performance imperatives has fundamentally altered sexual relationships. The unswerving neoliberal belief in the market frames it as the answer to all problems, including satisfying the individual's sexual desires (Hammond & Van Hooff, 2020; Rand, 2022). At the same time, every consumer culture is an outcome of the inextricable interweaving of economy and culture. In line with this understanding, this chapter has argued that the consumer sexual script of Israeli sex consumers associates the market ideology of neoliberal rationalization with the Israeli cultural signifier of the anti-*freier*, which has become a central repertoire of Israeli cultural identity.

While the desire to avoid being a *freier* is not exclusively Israeli, as was argued by Roniger and Feige (1993), the centrality of this sentiment in Israel calls for an explanation because Israeli society has always emphasized collective goals and individual self-sacrifice and has been critical of individuals pursuing personal desires and profit. The *freier* discourse signals that the golden years of collective efforts are gone. Roniger and Feige's analysis showed that the refusal to be a *freier* is an unequivocal refusal to create unity between the individual and the collective, thus symbolizing a criticism against the heroic model of the past and, by implication, a protest against the very demand to sacrifice oneself. The *freier* discourse thus creates a split between the national and private self. Nonetheless, even those who refuse to be *freiers* do not entirely give up collective values, and the national and private self can therefore exist simultaneously and dialectically, turning the *freier*/anti-*freier* model into a complex of contradictory evocative messages. The fear of becoming a *freier* is a cultural obsession among many Israelis regardless of involvement in the sex industry. It is the story Israelis tell about themselves to themselves. As a result, the *freier* constitutes a central symbolic arena of interpretative contest for Israelis trying to make sense of and shape their existence as Israelis.

The contradictory evocative messages of the *frier*/anti-*freier* model are also present among Israeli sex consumers. Analysis of their written sexual experiences reveals how consumerism is bound with self-sacrifice to the male collective. Thus, the consumer sexual script becomes solid evidence that, for Israeli sex consumers, the masculine anti-*freier* discourse reflects the importance they place on collectivistic ideals.

Contrary to the argument raised by many Israeli scholars, as discussed above, that contributing to the collective turns the individual into a tragic figure, a *freier*, this chapter highlights how the male community glorifies the individual self-sacrifice; while sacrificing oneself for others may seem like *freier* behavior in other social arenas, the community ethical code of "putting one's neck on the line" for the sake of others implies heroism and altruism. However, since the *freier* is an antithetical symbol of Israeliness, the Israeli sex consumer community warns its members against free riding since everyone will then treat them like a doormat, i.e., a *freier*. This demonstrates how the consumer sexual script mirrors the existential meta-comment on life in Israel and generalized allusions to the credulity of human nature. It impacts sex consumers' perceptions of sex workers and their fellow consumers, illustrating that every social interaction is measured according to the potential threat of humiliation.

Notes

1 The original Hebrew phrase used here is "lying on the fence," which means something entirely different in Hebrew than the English phrase, which describes the inability to take sides or decide on one course of action. According to Rosenthal (2005, p. 371), this Hebrew expression means "to risk and get hurt for the sake of the common good or another person." The origin of the phrase is the action of three soldiers in the Six-Day War (1967) who lay down on a fence during battle to enable their comrades to go over their backs. The phrase has, ever since, reflected doing something noble for the sake of others, even if this involves self-sacrifice, and has gained popularity in reference to various political and social events. I have chosen the translation "put your neck on the line," but other English phrases with a similar meaning might be "to take a bullet for the others" or "stick one's head above the parapet."

2 The original Hebrew phrase here translates as "free eater." For the sake of clarity, I have used here the English term "free rider," which has the same meaning as a person who enjoys another's generosity without sharing in the cost.

3 This quote is from the now defunct sex portal website, which was closed by the State Attorney's Office in 2017.

3 The Hunter Sexual Script

On March 24, 2013 a post titled "Theater of Dreams" was published in the Trash Talk Forum. The author of the post described a game he invented in which a sex worker's phone number is passed only between the members participating in the game. This was a unique request since the forums' rules at the time forbade the public sharing of all information details. However, in the "Theater of Dreams" game, the phone number is transferred secretly and privately and only to members who have "sworn" to the game's rules. Furthermore, the phone number can be transferred to the next member in line only after he publishes a detailed report of the sexual act with the relevant sex worker. Before starting the game, the game initiator requested that members wishing to participate swear to the rules in a "virtual pledging ceremony":

> To confirm final participation in the game, you hereby undertake to swear allegiance to me in front of the entire forum. I require each of you to write down what is written here: "I hereby swear allegiance to you that I will respect all the rules of the game and will not give any information to anyone who might reveal the identity of the lady mentioned above." And at the end of the text, you must write: "I swear!!!"

Despite choosing not to participate in the game, several members responded to game participants' ensuing sexual reports. For example:

> Dear friends, I would like to offer my humble appreciation in the form of a fire ceremony to the brave hunters facing bold action in unknown territories. May your oath be faithful, and may you return from your mission in peace.

> The round is not over yet. However, I salute the member who created this game for the successful hunt and for the game production that makes these sexual reports unique and memorable reading. At first, the whole ceremony and preparation seemed a bit ridiculous to me. However, I admit that with each sexual report, my opinion changes, and my curiosity for the following report grows. Kudos to all of you!

DOI: 10.4324/9781003128670-3

The choice of language here – fire ceremony, brave hunters, bold action, mission, unknown territories – reveals the interlink between hunting and militaristic jargon and how the metaphoric "hunt" has become what Ortner (1973) called an elaborating symbol. Under her seminal notion of "key symbols," Ortner defined the elaborating symbol as "providing vehicles for sorting out complex and undifferentiated feelings and ideas, making them comprehensible to oneself, communicable to others, and translatable into ordinary action" (p. 1340). According to Ortner, elaborating symbols can order experiences through their conceptual power which is played out in key cultural scenarios, namely, scenarios that imply modes of action appropriate to correct and successful living in a specific culture. Furthermore, elaborating symbols are often reflected in linguistic structures and metaphors, which, according to Livnat (2022), reflect the values and views of speakers of the same culture or subculture. This chapter therefore aims, based on these premises, to analyze how the storylines of hunting that Israeli sex consumers tell themselves and others about themselves through the written sexual experience serve as a performative action designed to ensure the illusion of control in a world they experience as full of dangers and embarrassment.

Analyses of the various hunting rituals reveal their collective nature and their role as essential sources for cultural patterns. These collective hunting storylines show how the pursuit of a successful "hunt" with its inherent rituals becomes the main object of desire. I thus claim that Israeli sex consumers' hunting rituals became socio-erotic liminoid rituals that are both relational and pleasurable. Turner (1974) suggested that liminal experiences in modern consumerist societies have been replaced by liminoid moments, namely, out-of-the-ordinary experiences, a "modern" break from normality. It is through this playful as-if experience that creativity and uncertainty unfold in art and leisure activities such as theater and sports. For Turner, the engagement in the liminoid becomes tied to the individual consumption of the out-of-the-ordinary as a commodity reflecting an individualized search for excitement at the spatial and temporal fringes of the social.

By adopting Turner's definition of the liminoid and seeing the "Theater of Dreams" game as an epitome of the hunting rituals of Israeli sex consumers, this chapter shows how the consumption of paid sex embodies socio-erotic experiences. In these experiences, the motif of hunting is what allows sex consumption to be associated with games that involve initiation trials, effort, discomfort, and risk – all seen as out-of-the-ordinary experiences. The hunt in these rituals is both the goal and the means. Furthermore, the socio-erotic liminoid hunting rituals evoke a sense of temporary communitas among community members. The entire community participates in the social drama of the sexual act, even those who chose not to participate in the "game" and are content with reading the sexual reports. These hunting rituals become a symbolic action expressing a person's understanding of himself within the world in which he lives. Hence, the sexual script of the hunter gives Israeli sex consumers a performative and theatrical platform on which to play out their imagined masculinity.

In the following sections, I first discuss the characteristics of hunting as a virile collective ritual. I show how the sexual script of the hunter, which mainly occurs in outdoor sex venues, is a mixture of intersecting character-istics from the universal dominant repertoire of hegemonic, heteronormative hyper-masculinity and Israeli hegemonic ideals of militarized masculinity. I then present the effect of the metaphoric language of hunting on sex con-sumers' perceptions: some see sex workers as the hunted animals, while oth-ers consider them the hunters themselves. I argue that sex workers are used as a screen for projecting sex consumers' tension and contradictions and a resource for (at least vicariously) resolving such tensions. After demonstrat-ing how the correlations between sex and hunting also relate to discussions about consuming meat, I conclude that the hunter sexual script suggests that the figure of the hunter has three interrelated purposes. It serves as a strategy to "revive" hegemonic and heteronormative masculinity, as both the reactions of men who feel under threat and their resistance to this feeling, and as a form of bonding with their fellow men. The hunter sexual script thus reflects how the consumption of paid sex is often a social drama that functions as a plat-form on which various power relations are played out and contested.

How is Hunting Related to Sex Consumption?

> For me, I think that, apart from the adrenaline, the hunt comes to satisfy some other side of my personality that is not expressed on a daily basis.
>
> (Street Forum, March 14, 2013)

Extensive literature has addressed how sexual consumption can fulfill and satisfy emotional needs (Bernstein, 2007; Earle & Sharpe, 2008; Katsulis, 2010; Milrod & Weitzer, 2012; Sanders, 2008, 2013). However, there is a lack of research on the performative and theatrical aspects inherent in paid sex consumption and its expression via written sexual experiences. The post quoted above reflects Israeli sex consumers' understanding of the metaphori-cal hunt as a channel to express the aspects of their personality that remain repressed in everyday life. Furthermore, this post, variations of which can be found in all the forums, is often accompanied by phrases drawn entirely from animality worlds: "I fucked her like an animal," "hunters and owls," "the girl is a wild animal," "she is a street cat," "she licks like a dog," "I felt like a rider grasping the horse's reins," "rangers," "the street is like a zoo," and others. This metaphoric discourse serves as what Gavrieli-Nuri (2010) called a "cultural code" – a set of values, norms, and beliefs that guide the members of a specific culture. Since metaphors reflect cognitive infrastructure in the speakers' minds (Lakoff & Johnson, 1980), placing a particular emphasis on this discourse makes it possible to understand how the hunter sexual script has become a linguistic and conscious structure, providing its members with a conceptual, moral, and emotional framework for discussion.

In recent years, the generalized theory of "women gather, men hunt" has been questioned by scholars, showing that hunting has not always been marked as a masculine pastime and does not remain a masculinized pastime in every cultural context today (Browder, 2009; Lindemann et al., 2022). Nonetheless, the popular image of hunting as a quintessentially hypermasculine practice and an arena in which men have historically been able to symbolically assert their masculinity remains dominant to this day. As a result, the deep association between men and hunting remains a familiar component of historical analytical frameworks, especially those investigating masculinity. Throughout history, hunting has been regarded as a rite of passage and a coming-of-age ritual that turns a boy into a man and, thus, an activity through which men have defined their masculinity (Bye, 2003; Fine, 2000; Littlefield, 2010; Littlefield & Ozanne, 2009; Loo, 2001; McKenzie, 2000, 2005; Smalley, 2005).

Smalley (2005) presented hunting as a "virile folkway" which allows men to recreate battlefield experiences and wartime relationships with other men. According to Bye (2003), hunting as an "archetype of masculinity" enables men to get closer to their roots by meeting nature and its forces. The hunt symbolizes man's quest for space to exercise his abilities and build his self-esteem. However, the stalwart image of the hunter as a prototype of ideal masculinity rooted in physical courage, endurance, the ability to survive in hostile terrains, the capacity for violence, and the impulse to explore new lands (Sinha, 2008) does not mean it is a solitary activity. Indeed, various scholars (MacKenzie, 2000; Sinha, 2008; Sramek, 2006) have pointed out the collective nature of hunting, especially among the nineteenth- and twentieth-century British imperialists in Africa and India. They asserted that hunting symbolized imperial dominance over the environment and was crucial in constructing British imperial masculinity. The connection between masculinity, hunting, and imperialism is also associated with militarist rhetoric. Since we are living in a "post-hunting" society (Fine, 2000; Hallagan, 2012) where there is no need to hunt to provide meat for one's social group, hunting has become a male-dominated recreational activity that recaptures profound battlefield experiences and uses militarist rhetoric (Smalley, 2005). Militarism helped to create the masculine image of recreational hunters (Lee et al., 2014), with the hunt involving a strong male comradeship forged in groups (Brandth & Haugen, 2006; Bye, 2003; Kheel, 2007; Presser & Taylor, 2011).

Unlike other cultures in which hunting gave men a ritualized way of ushering their sons into manhood (Smalley, 2005), Israeli culture does not have an ancient hunting tradition. According to Appel (2021), the subsisting forager style in Israel is problematic, especially regarding hunting, as it is mostly illegal and socially unacceptable even when rare permits are obtained. Additionally, much of the land in Israel is urbanized, and expanses of wilderness are rare.

According to a recent newspaper article (Perlman, 2021), there are three kinds of hunting in Israel. There is "interface hunting," which is managed by the Nature and Parks Authority in cooperation with the Ministry of Agriculture and local authorities and mainly aims to dilute wild animal populations. There is illegal hunting, whose estimated volume reaches 15,000 annual cases and mainly focuses on deer and bird species. The final category is hunting for sporting and leisure purposes: about 2000 hunters hold hunting licenses which allow them to hunt wild pigeons, mallards, and several species of wild duck.

While hunting practices may not be part of Israeli tradition or cultural history, Israel is known for its militaristic nature, which may explain the dominance of the hunting metaphor and its use as an elaborating symbol by Israeli sex consumers. Israeli culture, as discussed in Chapter 1, possesses many military characteristics; camaraderie, sociability, and self-sacrifice are significant motifs in Israel's heroic epics, and lifelong relationships flourish regardless of differences in social or political status. This is reflected in the militaristic jargon – target, mission, bravery, killing, comradeship, and others – prevalent in posts published in the sex consumer forums over the years. For example, on March 25, 2014, a community member posted a "successful hunt" guide for new community members, detailing seven stages. He called the first stage "preliminary preparation" and the second stage "the hunter":

> 2. The Hunter: In the movie *Terminator*, there is a segment where the Terminator drives in slow motion and looks for targets to eliminate. He looks left and right and searches. This is what the hunter is like when looking for a girl to hunt. The idea is to drive at 30–40 km/h and scan all the points where the girls are standing.

The following stages include negotiations that involve checking the woman's skin color and the condition of her teeth, coordinating expectations, and, finally, performing the sexual act. In a previous work (Lahav-Raz, 2020a), I presented curb crawling as a preplanned and calculated ritual for which consumers must prepare and apply screening practices. However, in this post, beyond using the written guide as a way of bonding with his fellow men, the consumer's correlation between hunting, sex, termination, and elimination presents hunting as a celebrated display of power and control over space and the female body. Furthermore, it manifests the art of killing and risking life as a central cultural motif, thus indicating the intertwining of the soldier and the hunter. In his wanderings after the woman, the hunter aims to "eliminate" her; as Luke (1998) showed, the hunter gains ultimate control over the animal and the space through killing.

The fluidity between hunting and sex rituals may not be surprising since hunting has always had an erotic nature. Armengol (2020) argued that men use the hunt as a "theatrical performance" of phallic power in front of and in opposition to other male hunters. Scholars have long recognized the sexual element in the act of hunting and the erotization of the hunted animals; indeed, hunting has been regarded as closely related to the predatory and heterosexual prominent sexual script in Western patriarchal society (Armengol, 2020; Brandth & Haugen, 2006; Bye, 2003; Gelfer, 2013; Luke, 1998; Sinha, 2008; Sollund, 2020; Sumpter, 2015). According to Luke (1998), hunting is doubly sexual as both a source of erotic enjoyment and an expression of masculine gender identity. Moreover, heterosexuality is explicit in the comparisons between men's hunting and sex to the point that it becomes difficult to tell whether hunting describes sex or sex describes hunting.

These blurred boundaries between hunting and sex can explain why men and women outside the sex industry often use hunting metaphors in courtship rituals. However, while courtship rituals may be understood as a fragile arena containing the fear of embarrassment, rejection, and failure, paid sex is seemingly free of these dangers due to its alleged explicit power relationship. Nonetheless, as Sanders (2008) demonstrated, sex consumers' involvement in the sex industry is not so different from relationships that occur outside of it. The hunting metaphor, therefore, indicates the similarity between sexual relationships outside the sex industry and sexual relationships within it. It also points to spatial characteristics and to the meaning sex consumers give to the area where the sexual act is performed.

While outdoor settings such as street-based sex work are usually viewed as "pure" economic exchanges, thus focusing on the exchange of sexual acts for money, research findings have suggested that the purchase of street-level sex embodies Armengol's (2020) "theatrical performance" which can both confirm and undermine the sense of manhood. Since hunting rituals are overrepresented in street-level sex work, I claim that, unlike other sex venues such as discreet apartments or brothels, the street can be easily associated with open and "wild" nature, especially in Israel, where wilderness is rare. Sex consumers can view others (albeit from the car) while engaging in sexual encounters, thus offering a liminoid moment of the out-of-the-ordinary theatrical experience that cannot take place indoors or in the consumers' daily lives:

> I've long been trying to hunt girls on the street... Up till now, I mainly went to discreet apartments, but I'm fed up with that. It's too expensive and boring. I need something new and exciting, like hunting on the street. I need some action.
>
> (Street Forum, April 22, 2015)

Sollund (2020) suggested that many men experience the gradual loss of arenas where they can perform traditional masculine ideals. For these men, hunting, which represents one of the last bastions where men can exercise traditional, hegemonic masculinity, becomes a way to compensate for a bygone era and a status to which they were previously entitled simply by virtue of being men. The example above points to the strength of the emotional experiences inherent in sex consumption in general and street-sex consumption in particular and their transformation into socio-erotic liminoid rituals that allow men to exercise heteronormative masculinity rooted in out-of-the-ordinary experiences.

Who is the Hunted Animal?

As stated earlier, the animal imagery of hunting inevitably enables sex consumers to collapse sex workers into non-human animals, making the analogy between femininity and animality. In many sexual reports, consumers detail the "technical specifications" of sex workers' bodies which are ranked and given a numerical score according to the consumer's taste. Their body parts are referenced in comparison to the physical characteristics of animals: for example, "horse's teeth," "chicken's skin," "horse's mane," "dog's ass," and others. They are, in addition, objectified and animalized by using beastly nicknames, such as "sex panthers," "battle foxes," "playboy bunnies," "a cow that refuses to retire," and "bitch." For example, a member of the Central Lobby Forum wrote a sexual report using both the Hebrew word for a female dog, *calba*, and the common English-language insult for women, "bitch":

> The girl goes to the roof to hide the money in her hiding place, and it turns out that there is a *calba* on the roof, barking like hell. We started with a blowjob to the sound of barking. It wasn't good, so I asked if we could start fucking. The bitch flew at me (not the one outside, the one I wanted to fuck) and started scolding me: "Why are you touching me?!!" In short, it was a crazy turn-off, and I couldn't perform. My dick was offended, and went to sleep. She tried to wake it up, and finally, it worked. For five minutes, I was pumping to the barking rhythm ("Who let the dogs out, 'who', 'who', 'who'?"[1]). The bitches were losing patience: the one on the roof was losing her mind, the one on the inside makes faces like, "come on, get it done already."
>
> (October 2, 2015)

Duvall (1991) argued that animals are often totemic substitutes for human characters that blur the boundaries between the natural and supernatural worlds. Following Duvall, I argue that the beastly nicknames serve as a screen for projecting sex consumers' tension and contradictions and a resource for resolving such tensions. In the report quoted above, the female dog and the human bitch merge in the sex consumer's mind and, thus, blur the boundaries between the symbolic and the real, between the inner mental world and the outer world of reality. While masculinity is often rooted in hunting wild animals, this quote shows that for sex consumers, the animal imagery associated with sex workers is often of domesticated animals, such as dogs. Luke (1998) suggested that the association with domestication results from ancient cultural institutions. For example, the term "husband" means both a woman's spouse and a man who manages livestock for reproduction, namely, controls the sexual and reproductive lives of cows and pigs to further his interests. Thus, the common use of terms such as "cow" or "dog" to refer to women shows either women's similar domesticated status or a cultural expectation that such subjugation would be appropriate.

Furthermore, according to Luke (1998), the specific use of the word "bitch" results from the ancient perception of breeders who treated the bitch or female dog as a means to a valuable, profitable, or prestigious litter. The word is also an insult for assertive women, expressing the hostility felt toward those members of domesticated groups who do not quietly assume their designated subordinate position. As such, the female dog, due precisely to its domestication, is seen to carry an even greater danger than a wild animal because she can, at any moment, reveal her "true" nature. The quote above thus reflects the writer's sense of threat and his subjugation to the whims of the sex worker who has the power to help him perform his manhood (via her ability to engage in sexual intercourse) but who can easily emasculate him.

This perceived sense of threat is also reflected in the following example. A member of the Sex Tourist Forum tried to warn other members of the forum about high-end Thai sex workers: "Don't even think about the direction of the high-end girls because they are battle foxes, intelligent businesswomen dressed as innocent playboy bunnies" (April 21, 2018). Beyond the domestication mentioned above, the reference to high-end Thai sex workers as "battle foxes" can be explained by the scholarly claim that fox hunting became an emasculated sport during British imperial big-game hunting (McKenzie, 2000; Shina, 2008). Since fox hunting suffered from varying degrees of plutocratic excess, urban decadence, industrial encroachment, and, for some, the presence of women, this claim relates to foxes' feminized and inferior nature. By contrasting "battle foxes" with "playboy bunnies," the writer hints at the underlying power of using animals as totemic substitutes for human characters: high-end Thai sex workers are only innocent in appearance (i.e., the popular image of the playboy bunny) but, in practice, have the power to "fight back" by exploiting and reversing the power dynamic. This supports Luke's (1998) argument that the hunting quest is all that matters as it provides a heightened sense of being through the exercise of power.

Having understood that hunting is all about exercising power, it is interesting to see that some sex consumers see sex workers as the hunters and themselves as the hunted animals. This association is especially true regarding sex workers abroad. This metaphorical inversion reflects both the argument put forth by scholars that hunting is not a masculinized pastime in every cultural context today (Browder, 2009; Lindemann et al., 2022) and the assertion that the hunting discourse serves as the reaction of men who feel under threat and their resistance to this feeling. For example, in a post published in the Sex Tourists Forum on July 24, 2017, a member stated:

> Sex workers in Kyiv are usually hunters looking for some sponsor. Everyone in the club will smile at you and even pat your hand as if they are inviting you. But don't forget they are hunters; you will pay for it.

This quote reflects the display of power rooted in hunting and the ensuing acquisition of knowledge about the habits of "animals" and good familiarity with the terrain. Since the consumption of sex abroad often involves strangeness, as the sex consumer does not know the space as well as he does in his home country, for Israeli sex consumers abroad, the figure of the hunter is associated with the one holding power. Chapter 2 presented the perception of sex workers abroad as "not *freiers*," namely, having the power to humiliate sex consumers by turning them into *freiers*. The same is true regarding the hunting metaphor: in their home country, sex consumers can see themselves as hunters, but in foreign lands, sex workers own the power of the interaction, leaving sex consumers powerless.

However, not all sex consumers are comfortable with seeing themselves as helpless and emasculated. In the Trash Talk Forum on Telegram, one member tried to warn another against sex workers who might try to hunt him down. The warned member was outraged by the comparison and wrote: "Hunt me?? As if I'm a poor and helpless mouse." The author of the original post replied:

> Prey can also be a noble doe. In any case, I had no intention of turning you into a poor mouse or something weak. Women who are being hunted are sometimes powerful and impressive. Hunting does not mean that the hunter is stronger than the hunted. It's a matter of trying to seize the opportunity.
>
> (April 19, 2021)

In addition to exercising power, the hunting sexual script is closely tied to the consumer sexual script described in Chapter 2: both are anchored in the Israeli cultural code of not being humiliated in the eyes of others. The fear of humiliation creates a constant struggle for survival in which the individual must seize the options in front of him and evaluate them accordingly so as not to end up losing or, as in the above post, being hunted. When one feels humiliated, the metaphoric discourse of hunting serves as a reaction to the feeling of being under threat and resistance to this feeling. It may explain why even women outside the sex industry can be perceived as hunters. This association is tied to the recent End Demand policy adopted in Israel. While this policy was enacted in 2018 and enforcement began in 2021, it was present in the public debate taking place in the two preceding decades, which affected sex consumers' feelings of threat regarding their involvement in the sex industry. For example, on July 12, 2017, a member of the Street Forum wrote:

You don't understand what's happening on Facebook. There is a feminist gang, and they start hunting and attacking anyone who starts writing in favor of the legalization, calling him a fornicator and a rapist. They tag the Israeli Police in his messages. In their closed groups, they ask each other if anyone knows him, and they start shaming him. The power is in their hands now, and they can ruin your life. The feminists on Facebook act as a terrorist organization. We live underground. It's like being a Jew in Nazi Germany, hiding in some attic.

The author's comparison between the feminist threat to sex consumers and the Nazi threat to Jews shows not only the centrality of the Holocaust and its depth as the founding trauma of Israeli society (Kidron, 2010; Yair, 2014) but also the immense feeling among sex consumers of being hunted, intimidated, and under constant threat due to the changing public discourse and the popularity of a radical feminist discourse that considers them to be exploitative. The power differences, whether exercised by feminists hunting sex consumers on social media or, as previously shown, by sex workers abroad hunting for their money, determine the perceived power balance. In the opinion of many sex consumers, the new End Demand policy deepens the "masculinity crisis" from which they suffer (Robinson, 2000; Rogers, 2007). For example, following the new directive that imposes fines for being in a public area of sexual activity or for engaging in sexual acts within the sex industry, a member of the Main Forum channel on Telegram wrote: "This new directive ruins men's lives! It's not enough that the state discriminates against us in all other fields, now they are coming at us with that (July 13, 2021)."

Robinson (2000) and Rogers (2007) argued that the shifting patterns of work, threats from others (women, working class, racial minorities, gender ideologies), and tensions over masculinity as physical strength versus self-mastery had led men to feel anxiety over the loss of virility. Since male power reproduces through crisis and resolution cycles (Robinson, 2000), the hunter sexual script serves here as reflective terrain for expressing both masculine mastery in the figure of the hunter and the fear of losing mastery of the world. The crossbreeding between the exhibition of power and the fear of having it taken away is intensified in outdoor sex venues. Since it is relatively easy to identify sexual acts on the street, consuming sex on the street was far more dangerous even before the implementation of the new policy due to police enforcement efforts.

Furthermore, the enactment of the Prohibition of Consumption of Prostitution Services Law during the Covid-19 pandemic reduced consumption rates, especially in outdoor sex venues, due to lockdown measures that involved the closure of businesses and activities deemed as non-essential or high-risk (Lahav-Raz et al., 2022). As a result, on the Sugar Daddy channel on Telegram, a member wrote: "It's not a problem to go to private girls, the police won't enforce the law, but don't go near brothels and street prostitutes" (June

1, 2020). The threat posed by the police, which makes the street a high-risk arena, has been identified by various scholars as having a significant impact on the behavior of sex consumers (Brooks-Gordon & Gelsthorpe, 2003; Della Giusta et al., 2017; Holt & Blevins, 2008; Kong, 2015). The thrill of hunting and the action around it, especially in "dangerous" arenas, turned the hunting rituals into a celebrated display of "reviving" hegemonic and heteronormative masculinity by overcoming risks and showing courage. However, to see it as one more arena of hypermasculine practice is an oversimplification. The hunter-sexual script also serves as a theatrical and reflective arena for men to vent their existential anxiety about losing their mastery of the world and being humiliated by others and, hence, emasculated.

The many examples of the crosstalk between hunting and heterosexuality presented thus far, which reflect that both institutions eroticize power differences, are also reflected in the various discussions among Israeli sex consumers that revolve around consuming meat.

Meat Lust

Since hunting has long been viewed as a hypermasculine practice, it allowed the product of the hunt – the meat – and its gendered allotment to be associated with masculinity (Gelfer, 2013; Rozin et al., 2012; Sumpter, 2015). Moreover, both hunting and meat consumption have a solid sexual subtext (Galfer, 2013), and thus the animal imagery embedded in the hunter-sexual script also generates an extensive metaphoric discourse among Israeli sex consumers regarding food, especially meat. The language itself is saturated with references to eating, whether directed or implied: for example, "there are people here who have *eaten* a lot of shit," "don't become a free *eater*," "I had a *hunger* attack," "a report hot from the *oven*," and others.

In many sexual reports, especially on sex consumption abroad, there is an emphasis on the food served on the premises and how the food quality impacts the entire sexual experience. For example, a member of the Sex Tourist Forum wrote of an unsuccessful sexual experience in one of the clubs in Berlin. He finished his report by writing:

> The food is shocking, disgusting chicken with no taste. Instead of cakes made on the spot, they serve basic store-bought cakes. There are no snacks like there used to be on the tables. In the past, the cook would ask me what I wanted and would make me special Uzbek rice. Now the food is at the level of a military base: half-cooked pasta, half-cooked mashed potatoes, and revolting soup.
>
> (November 10, 2017)

In contrast, a successful sexual report ended with the statement: "By the way, the food served are top chef's dishes and don't fall far from the most prestigious restaurants" (Sex Tourist Forum, July 20, 2017).

These sexual reports demonstrate the close connection between animality, women, food, and sex. The sociological and anthropological literature links food, especially meat and roasting, with superiority, masculinity, and power. Since eating meat is a symbolic act, there is a close connection between eating meat and physical, economic, political, and social power. Thus, the consumption of meat is used as a signifier of activity through which men have defined their masculinity (Adams, 2010; Avieli, 2011, 2013, 2018; Avieli & Grosglik, 2013; Buerkle, 2009; Gal & Wilkie, 2010; Nath, 2011; Parasecoli, 2005; Parry, 2010; Potts & Parry, 2010; Sobal, 2005; Stibbe, 2004).

Gelfer (2013), on the other hand, showed that while meat can function as a signifier of heteronormative masculinity, it might also serve as a way of engaging the non-masculine world in a violent and sexualized manner. For example, a member of the Street Forum published a post sharing with the community that he had met a woman who seemed like a good candidate for a long-term relationship. He expressed his confusion about whether to share with her his "hobby" of consuming sex. One of the members responded:

> You remind me of a friend who was a big carnivore. One day he met a vegetarian, vegan, or one of those ideological types of woman. She was even active in one of those organizations that fight for animal rights. She was amazing, but she set conditions for my friend: it was either her or meat. At first, she wouldn't kiss him if he ate meat. But before they moved in together, she demanded that he stop eating meat and ban any meat products in the house. Believe it or not, he agreed to give up meat and became a vegetarian. When we met for a barbecue, he would make vegetables and marshmallows on the side. To cut a long story short, with time, he started looking miserable. He started coming to me to eat meat secretly. He would make up all kinds of stories for her to satisfy his lust for meat, regularly walking around with a mouth spray in his pocket. He acted like a cheating husband. One day he broke down; he stopped at the supermarket and filled the fridge with meat, sausages, pastrami, and whatever else. She was shocked when she saw it, left him for a while, but finally returned to him. I could stop here, but just to satisfy your curiosity, I will tell you that they stayed together, and she even switched to eating meat. She still fights for animal rights but eats meat. Of course, I'm not saying that you should tell your girlfriend about your hobby; I don't believe she will accept it. But can you really abstain from "steaks"? As one of the members already wrote, it's certainly possible to combine one with the other, and one doesn't need to come at the expense of the other.
>
> (March 14, 2013)

The first association that came to this member's mind is that of men as carnivores, implying that men identify eating meat with masculinity and controlling nature while women are identified with vegetarianism and veganism.

This dietary difference is linked to society's dichotomous divide between masculinity and femininity (Sumpter, 2015). Adams's (2010) seminal work on the explicit connection between meat consumption and the sexual objectification of women revealed how meat is not just inherently bound up with masculine gender performances but also with patriarchy and sexuality. The language around meat and power is thus gendered: not only do men identify with eating meat while women identify with vegetarianism, but the masculine "meat" is considered the very essence of something while the feminine "vegetable" signifies passivity or even mental dysfunction.

In the previous report, the writer compared the friend who became a vegetarian to a man castrated by his girlfriend and even humiliated in front of his friends. Nath (2011) demonstrated that men who abstain from eating meat are viewed as less masculine. Others have shown that the more meat a person eats, the more masculine they appear to others (Rozin et al., 2012; Ruby & Heine, 2011; Sumpter, 2015), thus making him possess hegemonic masculinity (Nath, 2011). Therefore, in contrast to his friends who could display their virility by consuming quantities of meat at barbecue gatherings, the vegetarian friend had to stand apart from his homosocial group, emasculated by putting feminized products, such as vegetables and marshmallows, on the grill.

Furthermore, the writer's decision to articulate a moral dilemma about whether to share a sex consumption hobby with a partner by comparing collective displays of masculinity in the form of barbecue gatherings and feminine dishes, which also represent long-term relationships, shows the close connection between meat, masculinity, and national identity. Barbecues have been shown to symbolize a celebration of culture (Hamilton & Denniss, 2005), in light of which Avieli (2013) discussed the national meaning of the roasted meat enjoyed by most Jewish-Israelis celebrating the nation's Independence Day. By focusing on the relatively new ritual of barbecuing meat, he argued that roasted chunks of meat symbolize refined chunks of "Israeliness." Through barbecuing meat, Israeli men were found able to ratify and reproduce some of the key cultural elements of their Israeli identity: the question of power versus weakness, the desire to hold on to territory while facing the realities of a dense frontier, and the constant struggle over space in the region. Following Avieli, if Israelis are consuming their Israeliness through roasted meat, then Israeli sex consumers use the meat and barbecuing metaphor as a proxy for their masculine mastery of the world while expressing their core anxiety of losing power.

Finally, the use of meat consumption as a stand-in for affirming masculinity and the analogy between meat, masculinity, and the consumption of sex is not unique to the sex industry. A famous example in Israeli culture of the relationship between women and meat can be found in a documentary made with Eyal Golan, a well-known Israeli singer, in which he admitted to multiple marital infidelities (Shilon, 2008). He explained his affairs by saying: "How much steak entrecote can you eat? You need a slice of bread with chocolate every now and then. Or, vice versa, if you eat a lot of chocolate, sometimes you need a good entrecote." When asked which was tastier, Golan replied: "In this case, both are delicious." His comparison between women and different kinds of foods has become a key phrase in Israeli culture in recent years.

There are, however, differences between these two examples. The Street Forum post compares meat consumption with paid sex and vegetarianism with sex within the framework of a relationship; Eyal Golan compares sex acts with meat and chocolate – two dishes that need to be consumed in moderation. However, both examples allude to the close connection between sex and heteronormative masculinity and the exercise of power via meat consumption. This again demonstrates that sex consumption rituals, rather like barbecue gatherings where one can eat "a good entrecote," take place only occasionally, allowing them to be seen as socio-erotic liminoid moments that enable an exit from the monotonous daily routine.

To conclude, since the performativity and the consequentiality of language are instruments of social life (Katriel, 2020), the hunting sexual script reveals how hunting storylines have become socio-erotic liminoid rituals. While there is extensive literature on different sex consumers' motivations (Earle & Sharp, 2013; Hammond & van Hooff, 2020; Huysamen, 2020; Pitts et al., 2004; Milrod & Monto, 2012; Monto, 2000), none of it has addressed the theatrical aspect rooted in viewing sex consumption as a social drama offering a liminoid moment of creating an alternative reality. Just like hunting, which does not occur in a social vacuum and whose norms and values can change and evolve to new meanings in a post-hunting society (Nurse, 2015), sex consumption patterns should be examined according to the culture in which they are embedded. The hunter-sexual script gives Israeli sex consumers an interpretive terrain for venting their fears of losing power in front of their peers and sex workers and becomes the canvas on which the unsatisfied needs of men today are projected.

The hunter imagery, rooted in post-modern hunting rituals, resembles what scholars have identified as an antidote to the stresses of modern life, namely, a way to have an adventure and refresh and renew themselves (Fine, 2000; Lindemann et al., 2022; Smalley, 2005). According to these scholars, hunting has become an authentic hypermasculine leisure sphere where men can engage in homosocial activity on a male terrain – one of the few remaining in an increasingly feminized and integrated world. Sollund (2020) argued that, in a climate where many men experience the gradual loss of arenas where they could perform traditional masculine ideals, hunting rituals serve as a protest against the gender equality ideals that are promoted by the state.

In line with these understandings, the mythopoetic aspect of the hunter sexual script presented in this chapter solidifies how the metaphoric hunter mirrors the perceived causes, tensions, and contradictions involved in what Israeli sex consumers perceive as a contemporary masculinity crisis while also engaging in the crisis and offering a potential resolution. By turning the hunting storylines into rules of binding behavior of sacrifice and initiation rites, Israeli sex consumers can reinforce the myth of men as hunters and thus enact aspects of the idealized hegemonic masculinity and affirm themselves. At the same time, they use the hunter-sexual script to articulate their narratives, ideologies, motives, and, primarily, to express their fears of losing their ancient mastery of the world. In this way, the script reflects the three interrelated purposes of the hunting metaphor: a strategy to "revive" hegemonic and heteronormative masculinity, the reactions of men to the feelings of threat and their resistance to this feeling, and a form of bonding with their fellow men.

Note

1   This is a reference to the Bahamian jukanoo band Baha Men's song "Who Let the Dogs Out."

4 The Addict Sexual Script

On April 14, 2014, during a social gathering, I was asked about the progress of my research on sex consumers. After the meeting, Joy,[1] a friend who had attended the gathering, contacted me and asked to be interviewed for my research. Although the research focused on analyzing written sexual experiences in online arenas, I agreed to interview him, mainly because I sensed his urgency to share his experiences in the sex industry. During the interview, he conceptualized his former, long-term involvement in the sex industry in terms of sexual addiction. For example, when sharing his experiences in street-based venues, he said:

> So, when I was in the addiction, I lived from pleasure to pleasure. When one pleasure was over in my mind, I was already thinking about how to get to the next pleasure. But after a while, you do it because you are so afraid of not doing it, but you don't have these amazing experiences anymore. After a while, there's no payback, you don't get the joy, the pleasure, the excitement, but you are just so afraid of being alone. You'd rather a perfect stranger is in the back seat of your car than spend another moment alone with yourself, and right after, you feel like you want to go and crash the car on the highway because you can't believe you just did that: "How did I believe that again?"… A large part of addiction is that you feel like the whole world is against you, everyone is to blame for your problems, and you have the right to reward yourself. But, after you reward yourself, you feel crappy about yourself, so it must be others' fault, so then you get to reward yourself more, which is an endless cycle.

Throughout the entire interview, Joy described the cycle of addiction, which includes the emotional storm that, to a large extent, "attacks" and "hijacks" the mind and body and takes away the ability to be "normal," i.e., the ability to resist the burst of emotions and control them. After the sexual act and the excitement that lies, primarily in the sexual act's preliminary stages of preparation and not in the sexual act itself, he expresses feelings of emptiness. Hence, the physical outlet also leads to a mental outlet which fills the soul with emotions such as guilt, anger, pain, shame, humiliation, worthlessness,

DOI: 10.4324/9781003128670-4

loss of dignity, and remorse to the point that one cannot exist without the other.

Joy's conceptualization of sex purchasing as an addiction was not unique. In a post published in the Discreet Apartments Forum on September 12, 2015, a member wrote:

> Yes, I'm addicted to sex workers. I am a consumer because I'm addicted to the thrill of going to a sex worker. I will even go so far as to say that I would be happy if all sex workers stopped working in the field and prostitution ended because then I would have no choice but to quit this addiction. Just like a drug addict or a gambling addict who would be happy to have someone stop their addiction.

This quote highlights the thrill of going to sex workers as the leading motivation for involvement in the sex industry as consumers. At the same time, beyond the thrill, this quote points to the leading force of suffering that lies in addiction and the consumers' wish for an external force to help them stop the habit. As in the previous chapter's description of the metaphoric "hunt" becoming an elaborating symbol in Ortner's (1973) terms, so too the addiction storylines. The self-identification and pathologization as an addict, the attempt to give signs in the body, mind, and soul of the suffering associated with sex consumption, and the need for recognition and social legitimacy have gradually gained momentum among Israeli sex consumers who share their sexual experiences online. Moreover, under the auspices of the online community, the addictionology discourse (Lahav-Raz, 2022) that structures the mode of speech in a performative genre has normalized the experience of sex purchasing as an addiction to the extent that it has become the online community's key cultural scenario (Ortner, 1973).

In a previous work, I focused on the addict sexual script as a coping strategy that, while internalizing sex consumption as socially deviant behavior, also serves as a strategic practice for negotiating and challenging masculine hegemonic ideals (Lahav-Raz, 2022). In this chapter, I aim to develop this argument further and examine the addict sexual script as a symbol of hybrid masculinity (Bridges & Pascoe, 2014; Demetriou, 2001), i.e., men's selective incorporation of performances and identity elements associated with marginalized and subordinated masculinities and femininities. According to Bridges and Pascoe (2014) and Demetriou (2001), hybrid masculinities work in ways that not only reproduce contemporary systems of gendered, racial, and sexual inequalities but also involve the reformulation of hegemonic masculinity to make it seem less threatening. Adopting this theoretical framework can indicate how Israeli sex consumers distance themselves from traditional norms of hegemonic masculinity by describing themselves as weak men, emotionally expressive individuals, and victims who suffer tremendously from their addiction. This self-description notwithstanding, they fortify existing social and symbolic boundaries and thus often conceal systems of power.

I further show in this chapter how the selective maneuvering between hegemonic and counter-hegemonic performances is accomplished by combining two discourses of the self. Since "narratives of self draw upon broader, collective narratives, values, and scripts that imbue these personal stories with socially significant meanings" (Illouz, 2008, p. 173), I argue that the addict sexual script tells us two simultaneous stories of the self: the story of the neoliberal, psychologized, and private self located in therapeutic logic (Illouz, 2008) and the story of the national and political-collective self located in the emotional character of Israeli victim culture (Lomsky-Feder & Ben-Ari, 2007; Lomsky-Feder, 2004; Schori-Eyal et al., 2014; Yair, 2014; Zerubavel, 2002).

In the following sections, I first discuss how the addict sexual script, as a manifestation of hybrid masculinity, has become an elaborating symbol for Israeli sex consumers, enabling them to resist stigmatization as exploiters while sheltering under the protective shadow of the addict label. Moreover, identifying oneself as an addict allows a release of moral responsibility while venting fears and expressing neediness – characteristics that go beyond the accepted social expectations of hegemonic masculinity. Thus, "playing" the role of the addict enables a rejection of shame while creating intimacy between community members and offering moral and social recognition and empathy. I then present the proliferation of the online community as a "community of suffering" that combines the two discourses mentioned: the therapeutic psychological narrative and the national victim narrative. While the online community has become a supporting arena that helps people who experience similar "suffering" share their mental burden, there are nonetheless underlying dangers: for example, what happens when the individual decides to "sober up" from the illusion of addiction or when he no longer sees himself as a victim? These are manifested in two types of confession that characterize the community: the confession as a ritual of community purification and the confession as a ritual of disillusionment. I conclude this chapter by introducing the term "sex-emotivism," which lays the ground for examining how sex consumption repertoires, especially the addict sexual script, work as platforms for an emotional and therapeutic understanding of both the self and collective identities.

The Addict Self as a Manifestation of Hybrid Masculinity

I spent half a million shekels on sex workers. My life is over because of my addiction. In sports gambling, there is advertising [warning you] that it is addictive. It should be the same with paid sex due to its addictive nature. Society needs to change its perception of paid sex. Not everyone can get free sex; it's not available for everyone, so the sex industry should be legalized, not criminalized.

(Telegram, August 13, 2021)

There is an inherent discrepancy in this quote. The writer begins with the statement that addiction to sex consumption has ruined his life and that people should be warned about the industry's addictive nature. However, he concludes that sex consumption should nonetheless be legalized and not criminalized since not all men can experience free sex. This echoes Connell's claim (1995, 2005) that in a culture where hegemonic masculinity is predicated on the sexual conquest of women, men can feel emasculated by their inability to find a sexual partner. Beyond this discrepancy, it is necessary to understand this quote in relation to its accompanying social climate.

It has long been widely acknowledged that moral discourse plays heavily in sexuality policy (Brents, 2016), with the stigma attached to the sex industry affecting all of its actors who are perceived as debauched and sullied (Hammond, 2015; Weitzer, 2007). As a result, vast scholarly attention has been paid to the moral difficulties faced by sex consumers (Chen, 2017; Chu & Laidler, 2016; Horswill & Weitzer, 2018; Lahav-Raz et al., 2023; Prior & Peled, 2021; Sterling et al., 2018) and their attempts to morally justify their involvement in the sex industry (Hammond & Hooff, 2020; Lahav-Raz et al., 2023; Marttila, 2008; Prior & Peled, 2019). These moral justifications result from the regulatory framework concerning sex work, especially the framework that dominates the individual culture (Lahav-Raz et al., 2023). Thus, and as was mentioned in the previous chapters, during the past few decades, the view that paying for sex is a form of violence against women has increasingly gained currency in the Israeli public, professional, and social advocacy discourses (Lahav-Raz, 2020b; Peled et al., 2020). The active efforts made in the past decade by feminist organizations to attach shame and stigma to the sex industry and portray sex consumers as abusive and deviant have heightened the tendency of sex consumers to stress the normative nature of their actions (Lahav-Raz et al., 2023).

In light of this social stigmatization, I argue that the addict sexual script is an outgrowth of the perception of sex consumers as "morally incorrect subjects" (Stoczkowski, 2008, p. 349). This perception turns the addict sexual script into a strategy to regain self-moral value by shaking off the stigma of being men who commit immoral acts and who are controlled by an external force, namely, the addiction itself. Moreover, when they self-identify as addicts, the men confront the social stigmatization by constructing a hybrid masculinity to cope with and challenge hegemonic masculinity expectations. For example, on December 30, 2014, a member of the Discreet Apartment Forum asked for a recommendation for his first encounter with a sex worker. Most comments, such as the following, included a warning not to start due to the industry's addictive nature:

I suggest you don't start with it, especially if you've been fine up until now without it. Don't do it if it's a passing whim and just a desire to check it out and have fun. Don't pay for what you can get for free. After my first time with a hooker, I was drawn to it and became an addict. You need to know that paying for sex results in constant comparisons and hooking up with someone outside the industry seems like such hard work, so you prefer to pay and be done with it.

This quote again exemplifies that having sex is considered a normative act of manhood. However, it also indicates that consuming paid sex can result in the inability to return to having sex with someone outside the industry. Hence, involvement as a consumer in the sex industry mirrors the adversity involved in the social expectations of men, which results in the need to "be done with it," i.e., to cast aside the social demand to present proper masculinity by accumulating sexual experiences. Thus, by describing himself as an addict, the writer selectively enacts traits conventionally associated with both hegemonic and counter-hegemonic masculinities. He fulfills the social expectations of men to have multiple sexual encounters while expressing weakness and fragility – traits that deviate from hegemonic masculinity.

Alongside this common response, another member of the forum expressed a different opinion regarding involvement in the sex industry:

Don't listen to them. A man's nature is the desire to mate. This notion of living with one woman for 30 years doesn't work. It's an invention by women because that is how nature made them. You will find a "lover" and a relationship, but if you grow some balls over the years, you will go to sex workers. Even in this forum, the accepted opinion is that the situation is getting more complicated with lovers and becoming similar to the case with a legal wife or even worse (not to mention how much it will cost you). That's why it's better to have fun with sex workers. It's cheaper, fast, and diverse – exactly what a normal man wants. Like everything in life, the trick is not to overdo it and get addicted; keep a balance.

(December 30, 2014)

Beyond the legitimization of "having fun with sex workers" as being what "normal" men want, this quote highlights one of the crucial elements that connect addiction storylines and hybrid masculinity: the constant and delicate boundary work (Lamont, 2012) of defining the margins between what is considered normal masculine behavior and what is pathological. As in the case of the careful regulation of pleasure – i.e., encouraging the consumption of sex while avoiding overindulgence and addiction – so too regarding components of masculinity: one cannot present oneself as an emasculated and victimized man while giving up all aspects of hegemonic masculinity. Hence, the former two quotes, whether aiming to prevent the individual from consuming sex for fear of addiction or to normalize the male sexual drive, highlight the selective traits of both hegemonic, subordinate masculinities and even femininities but in a way that fortifies the existing social and symbolic boundaries of hegemonic masculinity.

Furthermore, as many scholars have shown, these quotes hint at how hegemonic masculinity is anchored in presumptions about men's explosive sex drive and preference for sexual adventure and pleasure without commitment (Joseph & Black, 2012; Kong, 2016; Lahav-Raz, 2020a; Sanders, 2008). As such, society expects men to desire, seek, and enjoy multiple sexual encounters. Failure to live up to these rigid sexual and gendered expectations can result in what Kimmel et al. (2013) called "aggrieved entitlement." Hence, the inability to have free sex can cause feelings of emasculation, shame, humiliation, and the perpetual pursuit of this masculine ideal (Connell, 2005; Messner, 1997). Concurrently, when portraying themselves as addicts, i.e., fragile men, they balance the sense of (masculine) humiliation and indignity in a way that represents themselves as nonthreatening. The addict sexual script thus becomes a compensation strategy for the potential humiliation resulting from their inability to perform hegemonic masculinity (i.e., get free sex) and their immoral acts in the form of paying for sex in a social climate that criticizes such an activity.

Moreover, the individual's internalization of sexual consumption as a "normal" male activity but, at the same time, a potential danger due to overindulgence and addiction is closely related to the masculinity crisis experienced by men today. While there is much disagreement among researchers about whether there is indeed a masculinity crisis (Heartfield, 2002; Itulua-Abumere, 2013; McLean, 2021; Robinson, 2000; Rogers, 2007), Scheibling and Lafrance (2019) showed that the different and contrasting cultural doctrines regarding masculinity result in men's need to negotiate and balance competing gender expectations. These contrasting cultural perceptions, internalized by society at large, reflect the inability to recognize the aggregation of sexual encounters as a potential cause of distress. For example, Joy reported that, despite his extensive experience in therapy over the years, none of his therapists pointed out that he had a problem concerning sex consumption:

> I've been in therapy for 15 years. I have been to both individual and couple's therapy. I always shared about my sexual acting out, but none of my therapists said I might have a problem and should consider attending a 12-step program. There is a sense that this [consumption of paid sex] is what guys do. What's the big deal? So I wouldn't say they encouraged me to do it, but they also didn't discourage me.

The obliviousness of Joy's therapists to the distress caused by the increased consumption of sex reflects the paradoxical social expectations of men who, while pushed into a sexual expression of their masculinity, do not gain social legitimacy and recognition when they express anxiety and pain as a result of these social expectations. For Joy, it was only in the 12-step program that he felt seen for the first time:

The first time I shared everything I've done with someone was with my sponsor. I remember sitting with him in a coffee shop and just crying. It was the first time I took a 500-pound gorilla off my chest, and this person didn't run away and say I was a monster. He just sat there and understood and said, "I've been there, done that. It wasn't your fault; you didn't know what you were doing." He gave me big hugs and told me he loved me.

The "500-pound gorilla" is Joy's tremendous, longstanding effort to conceal his inability to enjoy what others may consider a "normal" masculine activity. The more he tried to perform the dimensions of hegemonic masculinity, the more he became trapped in a vicious cycle of obsessive consumption, which resulted in suffering. The first time he revealed his secret suffering was with someone who guaranteed him moral and social recognition and empathy.

While, for Joy, the guardian angel was his sponsor, for Israeli sex consumers operating online and in a bewildering social climate, the online arena serves as their sanctuary – a place where they can express the pain they are experiencing and receive recognition from others. As I described elsewhere (Lahav-Raz, 2022), one way of dealing with distress and despair is to vent these feelings in the online community, turning it into a confessional space and a therapeutic self-help group offering social recognition and support for members' suffering. The online community thereby enables a feeling of shared fates and liberation from social norms and limitations, together with disclosure of shared shame and guilt. Being a member of a community of like-minded people who experience the constant fear of being excluded, judged, or cast out offers shelter from the stigmatizing gaze of the mainstream. Hence, by becoming a therapeutic self-help group, the online community helps members share the psychological burden of addiction with others who experience similar conflicts and demonstrate understanding without moral judgment. Furthermore, the selective maneuvering between hegemonic and counter-hegemonic performances, i.e., boasting about various sexual conquests while sharing their potentially devastating consequences, is also achieved by combining two discourses of the self.

Community of Suffering: When the Sufferer Self Meets the Victimized Israeli

As previously mentioned, the Israeli public discourse moved toward a view of sex consumers as immoral perpetrators of violence. At the same time, the consumers internalized this view and, as a coping strategy, increasingly exaggerated their role as victims suffering from their addiction. However, transforming the addict sexual script into an elaborating symbol of victimhood cannot be fully understood without turning the gaze toward the social and cultural discourses of the self in which it is bound. Illouz (2008), who researched the juxtaposition of psychology and self-help in American culture, reminded us that incompatible cultural frameworks can blend to produce a hybrid cultural system. She demonstrated that the language of psychotherapy left the realm of experts and moved to the realm of popular culture, where it interlocked and combined with various other American key categories, such as the pursuit of happiness, self-reliance, and the belief in the perfectibility of the self. Following this line of thinking, I now go on to show how Israeli sex consumers combine two discourses reflecting the sufferer and the victimized self.

The first discourse is rooted in the global therapeutic narrative of self-help. According to Illouz (2008), the language of therapy and therapeutic discourse became a formal and specialized body of knowledge and a cultural framework that orients self-perceptions and the conceptions of others. The therapeutic cultural structure translates into the micro-practices of telling one's life story, which now revolves around psychic suffering as an ongoing constitutive aspect of one's identity. This may explain why, over the years, many posts in the various forums discussed the physical suffering involved in sexual consumption. For example:

> So often has a short foray turned into a white night; you turn around constantly, and even though the terrain is dead, you always have the feeling that right here, on this turn, you will catch someone. The truth is that I had quite a few successes with this "method," but many times, after a night out, I need two days to recover. My hands hurt from the many movements on the steering wheel, my body loses balance, and I walk around like a zombie. This is the price of addiction.
>
> (Street Forum, July 29, 2012)

Indeed, numerous posts described bodily sensations of suffering that result from the endless sexual pursuit: hands that hurt from holding the steering wheel, a sore back from sitting for a long time in the car, muscle pains due to sleeplessness, and physical imbalance. As soon as one consumer complains about his soreness, others immediately join in, demanding acknowledgment of their own pain. Illouz (2008) argued that this need for acknowledgment results from the fact that the individual has become embedded in a culture saturated with the notion of rights. The articulation of "recognition" claims that one's private suffering should be publicly acknowledged and remedied. The need for recognition goes beyond physical suffering; thus, alongside the painful, tired, and weak body, Israeli sex consumers also highlight the mental load that may stem from addiction. It manifests in severe feelings of guilt, shame, and humiliation, following an endless cycle of mental and psychic suffering. For example, a member of the Discreet Apartment Forum shared that he cannot stop the habit of meeting with sex workers despite having met a partner he loves:

Dear friends, I am writing this report with tears in my eyes. I'm a piece of shit. I'm a man who constantly cheats on his girlfriend. I simply cannot stop it. Please help me!... I look up to God and ask him to make me stop going to these places. It doesn't help me. Please, I'm begging; help me get clean.

(June 25, 2015)

One of the members responded:

Do you really think that, in just one day, you can sweep the whole matter of escort girls under the carpet and never return to it? I doubt it. I understand you have someone, but I have also had many relationships with girls. However, nothing can compete with the feeling of butterflies in your stomach before going to an escort girl, especially if it's someone you're going to for the first time. I can't see myself stopping because it's simply impossible to stop once you start. Even with partners outside the industry, during sex, I imagine myself doing it with one of the sex workers I've been with.

(June 25, 2015)

These examples show how the addict sexual script could not have gained traction without the online community's active involvement and development into a "community of suffering." Israeli sex consumers use the online community as a safe haven for expressing their inner addiction struggles. In this regard, the online community is organized around common and shared suffering and constitutes a support group that grants social validation, recognition, and meaning to the suffering that sex consumers experience due to their addiction. The community thus legitimizes the continuation of victimhood and suffering, and the addict sexual script becomes a form of expression and an interpersonal imagination that serves as guidelines for thinking about oneself and one's relationships with others. Hence, in Illouz's (2008) terms, the addict sexual script becomes a performative narrative, which is more than a story because it reorganizes the experience while telling it. As such, this mechanism can transform suffering into victimhood and victimhood into an identity.

The victimhood consciousness embodied in the addict self not only results from the Western therapeutic narrative; it has also found its place in the unique character of Israeli victim culture, which has turned victimhood into one of its key cultural scenarios. Various scholars have shown Israeli culture as constituted by trauma, whether ancient or recent, historical or mythical (Lomsky-Feder & Ben-Ari, 2007; Lomsky-Feder, 2004; Yair, 2014; Zerubavel, 2002). This is exemplified in the extensive psychological literature depicting how Jewish Israelis' interlocking layers of historical victimhood, particularly the Holocaust and the Israeli–Palestinian conflict, have become an inseparable part of the shared narrative constructed in their collective memory of trauma

(Bar-Tal, 2007; Bar-Tal et al., 2009; Schori-Eyal et al., 2014). This historical victimhood was demonstrated in Chapter 3 in the quote comparing Israeli sex consumers to hunted Jews in Nazi Germany due to the current policy and the public climate, which looked to describe the sex consumers as imperiled by cultural injustices. Furthermore, the historical collective victimhood, which is based not only on an objective experience but also on its social construction (Bar-Tal et al., 2009), creates a siege mentality – a mental state in which members of a group hold a central belief that the rest of the world has highly hostile behavioral intentions toward them.

This siege mentality, demonstrated in Chapter 2's discussion of Israelis who fear being turned into *friers* by others and Chapter 3's discussion of hunting storylines as the reaction of men who feel under threat, is also present among sex consumers who pathologize themselves as addicts. The siege mentality depicted in the addict sexual script results from the perception of themselves as victimized by sex workers and due to being men in Israeli society. For example, a member of the Sugar Daddy Forum on Telegram posted that he had invited a sex worker to his house, and she had stolen money from him. Another member responded:

> Bringing a sex worker to your home is a mistake. Never bring someone home, and never use your real identity. You never know who she is and what her craziness is. This is not just a warning; it's the result of the suffering of many men who have fallen victim to cruel acts.
>
> (October 16, 2020)

Beyond seeing sex workers as a potential threat, many discussions, especially on Telegram, bemoan the perceived institutional discrimination against Israeli men and their inferiority in the face of existing legal systems that are perceived as prioritizing women. This is especially evident in discussions about marital issues, such as divorce and child custody. For example, a member of the Trash Talk Forum channel on Telegram shared his painful divorce experience:

> When my wife wanted a divorce, she went for counseling, and they advised her to report me to the police. I came home and got a call from a friend who warned me about it. When I got home, she started yelling at me and doing things to upset me. I entered the room, but she didn't stop and then started yelling at me for nothing. I went straight to the door, opened it, and went outside, and she shouted that if I came back, she would call the police. From that moment on, I didn't come home; I didn't see my son for several months before I was arrested.
>
> (March 9, 2021)

He immediately received empathetic messages from others in the community. One member validated his sense of victimhood:

When a woman in Israel goes to a lawyer wanting a divorce, the first advice is to file a complaint and keep the man out of the house. In Israel, there is an insane amount of false complaints by women, who turn us all into victims.

As mentioned earlier, collective victimhood is not necessarily based on objective experience but rather on its social construction. As such, while, objectively, marital relations in Israel operate according to Jewish religious law, which prioritizes men, Israeli sex consumers can perceive themselves as victims and claim deprivation of their rights. This reversal of power relations, even if only imagined, is a consequence of the popular Israeli trauma discourse, which, according to Yair (2014), derives from a deeply ingrained and traumatic cultural worldview that connects four distinct layers: the mythological predicament of exile and persecution, historical evidence about attempts to attack Jews and Israelis, contemporary threats on Israeli security, and a sense of future illegitimacy. This multilayered cultural worldview constitutes a significant facet of Israeli national character, namely, its chronic existential anxiety. The trauma or post-trauma serves as a cultural code that Israelis use to explain their self and the national predicament. Accordingly, Israeli sex consumers are constantly preoccupied with finding out who has the potential to threaten them, whether sex workers or women in general.

Regarding the sense of masculine victimhood, sex consumers' perception of themselves as victims is an outgrowth of the public climate created by Israeli men's organizations over the last decade. These organizations have sought to entrench public awareness of what they see as masculine discrimination in the form of various laws concerning both the sex industry and family arrangements. For example, the Ministry of Fathers,[2] an umbrella organization that unites 20 different Israeli men's organizations, states in its membership campaign: "We are a group of fathers and men who have undergone crises regarding family, health, livelihood, and dealing with state authorities." They promote the perception that the state deprives many Israeli men of their rights despite them being the primary bearers of the livelihood burden and maintaining the state's security by serving in the military. According to the Ministry of Fathers, Israeli men suffer tremendous hardships, such as:

False arrests and imprisonments, loss of livelihood due to false complaints, maltreatment by the system and writs of execution, disconnection from their children, inability to exist with dignity and raise their children, inability to face the discrimination and racism that is directed toward them just because they are men who got divorced.

Hence, according to their perspective, divorce proceedings turn Israeli men into "victims of a system built against them decades ago." It thus becomes apparent that the Israeli siege mentality, which creates victim consciousness and is anchored in the belief that the rest of the world has highly hostile behavioral intentions, also pervades the self-perceptions of sex consumers in various aspects of their daily existence as both sex consumers and Israeli men. In this process, the online community serves as a space for venting and legitimizing the sense of victimhood and the victims' suffering. In other words, the online community helps create intimacy and social solidarity between members and serves as a fundamental common denominator many people can identify. This is highly valuable in a conflictual society such as Israel, where, as Lomsky-Feder and Ben-Ari (2007) showed, everyone is a traumatized and suffering individual.

However, this social solidarity is only solid as long as all community members perceive themselves as the only victims in their relationship with sex workers. When certain members decide to "sober up" from the perception of themselves as addicts and to "get clean," social solidarity is in danger of collapsing. Delicate boundary work (Lamont, 2012) distinguishing between sharing and disillusionment is, therefore, necessary to avoid such a threat. This can be illustrated by two types of addictionology confessions: a ritual of community purification and a ritual of disillusionment.

Addictionology Confessions

> When you walk around so much among the wretched things of life, you are exposed to a lot of garbage, sometimes you even smell it, and you try very hard not to get dirty and wet from the juice. The problem starts when you start sorting through the garbage (for better or worse) and no longer cover your nose because you have already gotten used to the smell.
>
> (Street Forum, March 3, 2013)

Using trash epithets as a way of describing sex workers and the sex industry results from moral perceptions that define some social groups, such as the indigent, refugees, and migrant workers, as human waste, a liminal population, and hence, a threat to the stability of social and national boundaries. When sex consumers decide to "sort through the garbage," they risk adopting a reflexive lens which may lead to sobriety from the illusion of addiction and recognition of the cost of their actions on themselves and their sexual partners. This exposes the two practices that characterize the online confessions of Israeli sex consumers who pathologize themselves as addicts. The first type of confession is a ritual of community purification in which a member can confide with others about his addiction. This type of confession helps to absolve the individual from moral responsibility for his actions. For example, when one member shared with others his suffering and his unsuccessful attempts to "get clean," another member responded: "I support you in your coping and the inner battles awaiting you. Unfortunately, your weakness will cause you inner struggles. Good luck, brother" (Street Forum, May 18, 2015).

This type of confession, followed by community members' comments, serves as a purification ritual since the confiding individual makes a double move. First, he declares himself a weak man who submits to the power exerted on him and thus frees himself from responsibility for continuing the cycle of suffering. Second, he offers members who read the confession a sense of relief and a communal moral affirmation that what they experience is not an individual pathology but a shared experience of suffering. Hence, this type of confession enables a sense of shared fate, liberation from social norms and restrictions, and a venting of feelings such as shame and guilt. In other words, the ritual establishes the community solidarity myth. From the moment of confession, the individual is not only comforted and freed from admonition and ostracism, but, as Bauman (2013) showed, his private problems are presented as worthy of public discussion. As such, an individual pathology is normalized as a standard masculine act.

Furthermore, this community purification confession serves as a morality play in which the main plot is a struggle between the good and evil forces in the human soul and the externalization of the internal struggles to get rid of the demons that endanger one's soul. This way, one can continue in an endless cycle of consumption-confession-purification-consumption while bearing the burden of addiction together with like-minded others. In this process, expressive writing helps the suffering individual adapt to pain.

Contrary to the feeling of normalcy gained in this community ritual, the second type of confession is more of a ritual of disillusionment. While the community embraces and comforts the former, the latter, in which the addicted individual embraces a reflective lens toward himself and others, is subsequently blasphemed and ostracized. The individual seeks to be cleansed of his sins and suffering while demanding that others take responsibility for their actions. Consequently, this type of confession holds up a shameful mirror to sex consumers' behavior:

I'm here to tell all those looking for an escape – it exists! For years I tried to quit, but the satisfaction I found on the street, I couldn't find in other places. I realized that I was blind, motivated by fear. Things that scared me in the real world didn't exist on the street. In the street, it was a complete sexual conquest. I was in control. I haven't visited a sex worker in a year and am convinced I will never do it again! You have all loved once, and you know deep down that in every encounter with a sex worker, there is always a place in your heart where you wish it could be different. And it's possible. That's what I'm here to tell you. You need to understand that you are taking advantage of a girl in the most fragile state of her life. This momentary satisfaction will fade and become a hole in the wallet and heart. There is an alternative! A different side of life. The side that lives not only when there is love but when there is desire. A desire to learn, a desire to travel, a desire to see, a desire to sleep even... I knew I was lost in a world that didn't let me go for a moment. Every night was another opportunity. And I'm free, friends, I'm free.

(Street Forum, March 3, 2013)

While this post illustrates the practice of a person who has undergone a spiritual revelation and become enlightened, this ritual of disillusionment prompted a severe reaction from other community members who felt judged:

You hurt me. You cleared your conscience while spitting into the well we all drink from. You are the wisest who has received enlightenment; we are blind and rapists. You are alive, and we are dead. Now suddenly, you pull the card of "being with a sex worker is exploitation and humiliation of the woman's body?" It's hypocritical... Talk to us in a few years; I bet you'll be back.

(Street Forum, March 3, 2013)

While in the ritual of community purification, community members can read the confession and receive a sense of relief and normalcy, in the ritual of disillusionment, instead of being viewers, they become viewed and ostracized by the confessing individual. Hence, the experience of self-reflection is wrapped in shame since turning the gaze "to the other side" also means acknowledging participating in shameful and unjust acts. As such, community members rarely use this type of confession to reflect upon themselves:

I admit I'm mostly blind to the other side. The ability to look and see what is happening on the other side....I hardly see anything else. I'm afraid to delve into these thoughts, and like any addict, the desire to get laid is stronger.

(Street Forum, March 3, 2013)

Amir (2008) claimed that shame signifies awareness. For her, shame is the first form of reflection since it is a way of observing ourselves through the imaginary eyes of the other. When a community member reads a disillusionment confession, he is given the opportunity to see how others may perceive him. According to Hazan (2008), the process of monitoring shame is not only a mechanism for self-regulation but also carries a certified distinction between good and evil. When one decides, by his confession, to breach the bond of silence, it jeopardizes the group solidarity ethos and what members perceive as a natural social order. In that process, the confessor's shameful glances become guilt, and, as Amir (2008) asserted, while shame and guilt are intertwined, they are, at the same time, separate. Shame perceives the other as an object, while guilt considers the other a subject. Feeling guilty means looking at the other as ourselves while feeling shame means looking at ourselves as the other.

Furthermore, understanding how guilt and shame are intertwined helps us understand why, in disillusionment confessions, many metaphors revolve around sight and blindness or life and death. Blindness here becomes a conscious choice, a practice aimed at protecting mental and moral conscience. As stated earlier, the more you feel like a victim, the less you feel empathy toward others; choosing blindness frees oneself from the need to see others as subjects and allows the continued denial of personal responsibility necessary to preserve victimhood consciousness.

The addiction storylines presented in this chapter perform a hybrid masculinity that combines not only hegemonic and counter-hegemonic traits of masculinity but also harnesses two stories of the self. The jointure of the neoliberal psychologized private self located in therapeutic logic and the national and political-collective self located in the emotional character of Israeli victim culture presents the addict sexual script as a platform of sex-emotivism. Applying the line of thought outlined by Grosglik and Lerner (2021) in their study of gastro-emotivism, which showed the verbal ways in which emotions are expressed, explored, and navigated in the popular TV show *MasterChef Israel*, I show how the addict sexual script points to the overlap between the masculine self and the broader Israeli cultural narrative of the self. In other words, to fully understand why Israeli sex consumers choose to pathologize themselves as addicts, it is vital to comprehend the blending of cultural frameworks into a hybrid cultural system. As an elaborating symbol, the addict sexual script combines emotional and therapeutic culture with the victim narrative that characterizes Israeli society. The powerful symbolic capacity of sex consumption to represent both the self and Israeli collective identity uncovers the merging between emotional-private and political-collective modes of expression in public culture regarding sex consumption. This is especially relevant in a social climate that made sex consumption illegal and thus bewildered the consumers. The addict sexual script thus became a coping strategy that allows Israeli sex consumers to unite various and diverse practices that combine traits of hegemonic masculinity with "sensitive" and victimized masculinity. Israeli sex consumers perceive themselves as victims of social stigmatization due to sex work policy, victims of a contradictory set of masculine expectations, victims of state discrimination against them as Israeli men, and, above all, victims of their addiction. Thus, sex-emotivism in the form of the addict sexual script allows us to trace the diffusion of the language of psychology and how the discourse of addiction illuminates the way Israeli culture works.

Furthermore, it reflects how addiction storylines harness cultural systems for self-improvement without a trace of moral guilt and shame. While sex consumption can serve as an escape from the hardships of life, it simultaneously incorporates the social stigma against the consumption of commercial sex, which leads to a constant need to gain social recognition from their peers for the adversity imbued in their addiction. When receiving community validation and a sense of normalcy, sex consumers can tie themselves to the social and cultural discourse of disease while enjoying the protection of the addict and pathological label.

To conclude, the flourishing addictionology discourse of Israeli sex consumers teaches us how cultural artifacts can be translated and assimilated into local cultural contexts; it reflects changes in the collectivist basis of Israeli culture, which moved toward a global individualistic and consumer culture (Ram, 2013) in which therapeutic rhetoric dominates all areas of life. However, the individualization of Israeli society (Kaneh-Shalit, 2017) does not eliminate the shared basis of Israeli society as a society that perceives itself, first and foremost, as a victimized culture. The contemporary manifestation of this communicative style is the addict sexual script which has become an attractive and effective communal mechanism for presenting the self.

Notes

1 A pseudonym he chose for himself.
2 https://www.drove.com/campaign/5e74d3fee591e30001deb13f?utm_medium =copy+link&skey=.27ux (Following quotes are all from this campaign site.)

5 Moving Beyond the "Client"

In 2005, Laura Agustin (2005) opened a window into the culturally situated work of the sex industry. She argued that societies' twin reactions to commercial sex – moral revulsion and resigned tolerance – have, paradoxically, enabled its uncontrolled development in the underground economy and impeded cultural research. Agustin called for a cultural study approach that looks at commercial sex in the widest sense, examining its intersections with various social strata, such as race, class, gender, identity, citizenship, and other social trajectories of life. Adopting Agustin's (2007) understanding of the way in which the meaning of buying and selling sex changes according to the social, cultural, and historical processes in which the transactions are situated, this book has focused on sex consumption patterns and their myriad connections to the fabric of everyday Israeli homosociality. In other words – and paraphrasing the anthropologist Clifford Geertz (1973, p. 448) on culture as "the ensemble of stories we tell ourselves about ourselves" – the book has explored the sexual stories that narrators tell themselves about themselves and their construction of their heteronormative masculine self. And, beyond the private story, it also asks what these sexual stories tell us about the connection between Israeli masculine components and their impact on sexual buying patterns.

Considering that technology, culture, and consumerism are inextricably intertwined, this book has looked at the commonly written representations in various digital environments and how they mirror the different ways of being an Israeli sex consumer. Namely, what do sex consumers write about their sexual experiences, and how do they juxtapose their masculine identity with Israeli society's various central cultural motifs? This conjunction reveals the dynamics of sex consumption patterns and the constant negotiation of local and global masculine characteristics. All three sexual scripts presented thus far – the consumer, the hunter, and the addict – permeate universal masculine scripts: consumer-culture rationality; hegemonic masculinity, heteronormative masculinity, and hypermasculinity; and the neoliberal, psychologized, and private self located in a broader therapeutic logic.

These sexual scripts are, at the same time, heavily bound by localized cultural scripts of Israeli masculine characteristics. While my analysis of anonymous sexual stories has undoubtedly prevented me from addressing

DOI: 10.4324/9781003128670-5

Israeli identity characteristics such as ethnicity, nationalism, religion, and social status, it has allowed me to represent authentic knowledge formulated and uniquely expressed by the individual sex consumer. Hence, even though these critical elements are missing from the analysis, the compound sexual stories reveal their interconnectedness to current popular representations of canonical veteran images of Israeli identity. These include the cultural fear of becoming a *freier*, the militarized masculine self, and the Israeli sense of victimhood. The book's analysis therefore generated two main outcomes. First, it shows that to understand sex consumption patterns and rationality, one must pay attention not only to sex consumers' motivations, personal characteristics, and venue preferences but also to the interwoven and ingrained connection between local cultural characteristics and universal dominant discourses regarding sexual consumption. Second, it shows that to understand the national character and the masculine identity that characterizes Israeli culture, one must examine the masculinity patterns of its sex industry consumers through their sexual scripts.

My springboard for discussing the consumption of sex in the digital age and the construction of Israeli masculine sexual scripts was Gagnon and Simon's (1973) seminal work on sexual script theory. As argued in Chapter 1, research on sex consumption in the digital era should move beyond simplistic understandings of "the client" as a heuristic category. The interactionist perspective on sexual scripting developed by Gagnon and Simon (1973) highlights the dominance of specific heteronormative practices of sexual scripts. It recognizes the mechanisms through which sexual scripts are reproduced and can be negotiated and questioned within broader universal and local changing configurations of gender, sexuality, and, I add, culture.

In the previous three chapters, I showed the multiple ways in which these sexual scripts are reproduced, negotiated, and questioned by drawing on various social, cultural, and material resources. In this concluding chapter, I use Boltanski and Thévenot's (1999, 2006) theory of cultural sociology of worth to understand the cultural formations of masculine identity and men's performance of multiple identities when engaging in sexual commerce.

Sexual Scripts as Moral Justification Regimes

While I eschew definitive moral judgments about sex consumption, I found Boltanski and Thévenot's (2006) cultural sociology of worth, which concerns how people actively navigate moral systems, to be a useful theoretical lens through which to examine the negotiation and maneuvering between the different sexual scripts performed by Israeli sex consumers. As previously stated, "morality politics" plays heavily in sexuality policy, especially in sex work governance (Harrington, 2018; Pitcher, 2019; Weitzer, 2020). This is also the case in Israel, where an End Demand policy was adopted in 2018. Society's moral revulsion toward the sex industry and sexual commerce results in a stigmatization which impacts all of its actors, who are perceived as debauched and sullied (Hammond, 2015; Weitzer, 2007). Having a discredited and "spoiled" identity (Goffman, 1963) or being a "morally incorrect subject" (Stoczkowski, 2008), compels individuals to assume the responsibility of managing their interactions to prevent others' discomfort while preserving their sense of moral self-worth.

Boltanski and Thévenot (1999, 2006) accentuated the preservation of one's moral self-worth as moral justification regimes. They claimed that individuals adopt different frameworks of moral reasoning, namely, justification regimes which operate as logics defining which actions and arguments will grant them moral worth. According to this view of pragmatic morality, moral worth is flexible, and moral practices are fluid and context-specific: some rationales and values have meaning in one context, and some acquire meaning in others. To achieve moral worth, individuals operate according to the situation and regularly apply their agency to switching between different justification regimes.

Following in Boltanski and Thévenot's pragmatic morality footsteps, I argue that the consumer, hunter, and addict sexual scripts are neither rigid masculinity models nor personality types but rather thinking tools. All three sexual scripts serve as moral justification regimes, namely, flexible frameworks available to consumers in different contexts. These contexts may be geographical. This was demonstrated in the cultural motif of the Israeli *freier* as a manifestation of consumer cultural rationality in which sexual experiences abroad were organized through the attempt to avoid being a *freier* while indicating Israeli consumers' frustration with their constant humiliation at the hands of Israeli sex workers. The contexts can also be spatial, as demonstrated in the elaborating symbol of hunting and the popularization of collective hunting storylines expressing hypermasculinity and militaristic jargon as liminoid rituals, especially in outdoor sex venues. Moreover, the moral justification regime can be closely linked to the imagined audience reading the sexual story. This was demonstrated in the addict sexual script and Israeli sex consumers' use of the addict label as an elaborating symbol of victimhood – a compensation and sheltering strategy in front of their community peers and society at large to resist stigmatization as exploiters.

Finally, and as I showed elsewhere (Lahav-Raz et al., 2023), moral justifications also result from the regulatory framework concerning sex work, especially the framework that dominates the individual culture. In her groundbreaking essay, "Thinking Sex," Gail Rubin (2002) reminded us that what is understood as sexually deviant is always culturally and politically defined. Thus, the growing international legislation to outlaw prostitution and the significant shift toward abolishing, restricting, controlling, or containing sexual commerce as the preferred strategies for governing commercial sex have impacted Israeli sex consumers' moral reasoning. Thus, the struggle over recent decades to criminalize Israeli sex industry clients and the use of punitive law enforcement to achieve this have turned them into deviant and morally incorrect subjects. This has increased their stigmatization and forced them to maintain their moral self-worth.

As stated, I am not arguing here that these sexual scripts are stringent; rather, I see them as somewhat flexible. By using these sexual scripts as a moral justification regime, Israeli sex consumers negotiate their self-image and sense of belonging to Israeli culture. The flexible switching and maneuvering betwixt and between different scripts and contexts reveal how they all serve as discursive strategies drawn from diverse and integrated global and local cultural frameworks, turning them into various cultural repertoires of heteronormative homosociality. In Swidler's (1986) terms, they become part of a meaning-making "toolkit" of habits, skills, and styles from which people define themselves and their relationship with others while constructing action strategies. These discursive strategies are fluid and can be used differently and in diverse contexts; however, they all have one thing in common: their aim to ease discomfort in front of society's judgmental gaze upon sex consumption. This book shows that, when involved in controversial market commerce such as the sex industry, the chosen sexual script becomes a moral shield. This defense strategy enables individuals to challenge social hierarchies and seek dignity. Sexual scripting thus clusters many meanings and teaches us that the construction of male identity intersects with other discourses related to both sexual consumption as a morally tainted activity and a person's culture; it turns the rigid notion of "masculinities" into a more flexible terrain of situated social and cultural practice.

Furthermore, when sex consumption is perceived as a morally tainted activity, the maneuvering between different justification regimes echoes the constant moral boundary work (Lamont & Mizrachi, 2012) that individuals conduct to differentiate themselves from others and produce their moral self-perception. According to Lamont and Mizrachi (2012), boundary work is the cognitive practice of interpreting classification categories to define social groups and mark the limits of belonging through which people distinguish themselves from others. Hence, understanding responses to stigmatization requires considering the formation of collective identities: how "us" and "them" are mutually defined and how individuals and groups engage in boundary work when responding to stigmatization in both private and public.

Applying pragmatic analysis (Lamont & Thévenot, 2000) and Lamont's (2009) conceptual lens of boundary work on Israeli sex consumers' written rationalities, it is interesting to see that beyond the somewhat expected moral boundary work between consumers and sex workers or between the individual and society, all three sexual scripts have demonstrated an obsessive preoccupation with the component of Israeliness. Israeli sex consumers often use their Israeli identity to distinguish themselves in front of the world. In this way, Israeli male identity with its multitude of masculine characteristics – such as hypermasculinity, camaraderie, sociability, the willingness for self-sacrifice, straightforwardness, the constant fear of becoming inferior, and an eternal sense of victimhood, to name just a few – is also revealed as the initial departure point from which the individual tells himself and others his story. Hence, while sex consumption is not a unique Israeli masculine performative act, the three sexual scripts become moral logic anchored in the broader moral logic of Israeliness. Israeli culture is therefore seen as not only a barrier but also a repertoire for creative solutions that integrate these discursive formations and conceptualize them as a boundary work that simultaneously produces a way to connect (to "us," namely, Israeliness) and a way to differentiate (from "them," namely, not Israelis).

When thinking reflectively about this book – whose research was carried out over different and prolonged periods in which not only the technological affordances and legislative governance but also my own perspective changed – what became clear was that masculinity within sexual commerce is fluid and context-specific. Moreover, a profound understanding of sexual commerce patterns demands the consideration of both universal or global discourse on masculinity and the more canonical veteran images of a specific culture. Despite this being a peripheral case study, in an attempt to contribute more broadly to a scholarly understanding of masculinity, consumerism, and digital capitalism, I would like to suggest a new theoretical concept of "communitext." In the following concluding remarks, I use this concept as a model for thinking about sex consumers' online communities and how they create a situationally constructed form of homosociality. It thus contributes both theoretical and empirical perspectives to the broad discussions of paying for sex in the digital age and the construction of masculinity as a homosocial rite of passage.

Communitext

Throughout the book, I examined written sexual stories of sex consumption on two digital platforms: a sex consumers' online community created on an online sex portal and a community of consumers created on different Telegram channels. Although the former still exists, recent sex work governance banning sex industry-related publishing has damaged its popularity. This has resulted in a mass migration of sex consumers to platforms like Telegram which are characterized by greater privacy as the author himself can delete threads. While these two digital platforms undoubtedly differ from one another and have divergent architectural affordances, they both serve as what Tiidenberg and van der Nagel (2020) called "sexual social media" where people can consume, create, and interact sexually. As such, they are increasingly involved, directly and indirectly, in producing, consuming, mediating, and exchanging a wide range of sexual services (Swords et al., 2023). This turns them into what Schwarz (2010, p. 639) called "technologies of arousal." Sexual media platforms have thus become a key site for forging sexual subjectivities, radically transforming how sexual relationships are understood, experienced, and narrated (Gilroy & Kashyap, 2021; Tiidenberg & van der Nagel, 2020).

The understanding of how digital technologies and platforms function as novel pathways and infrastructures for political, cultural, and economic life and shape modern sexualities (Adams-Santos, 2020) has recently attracted much scholarly attention to various aspects of sex work platformization (Cowan & Colosi, 2021; Duffy & Meisner, 2023; Hardy & Barbagallo, 2021; Swords et al., 2023; Velthuis & van Doorn, 2020). However, without denying the importance of understanding the risks and potential of sex work platformization, this pervasive focus not only overemphasizes the affordances of internet-based sex work to the point of ignoring the dangers that emerge online (Jones, 2015) but also neglects the early literature on text-based communities and their contribution to various aspects of identity construction. Moving on from the relatively circumscribed "pleasure/danger" analytical framework and following the understanding that sex consumers' text-based communities are still highly popular due to the anonymity they offer, I want to focus here on the ability of sex consumers to share mutable, reflexive, performative, and socialized sexual stories. These accumulated sexual stories turn the digital environment into what I call "communitext," which contains various practices of consuming, creating, and interacting sexually that result in intense feelings of cultural intimacy.

The "communitext" theoretical concept combines the community's emphasis on different textual configurations to deliver information and emotions with Turner's (1969) concept of communitas. Turner, who defined the anthropological usage of communitas, was interested in the interplay between social "structure" and "antistructure." When referring to the liminal, Turner showed it as an antistructure moment: a "moment in and out of time, and out of the secular social structure, which reveals, however fleetingly, some recognition (in symbol if not always in language) of a generalized social bond" (1969, p. 360). In this unstructured liminal moment, all community members are equal, allowing them to share a common experience, usually through a rite of passage which brings about a state he calls "communitas." In other words, communitas emerges where social structure is not. Thus, communitas, as a characteristic of people experiencing liminality together, not only denotes intense feelings of social togetherness and belonging, homogeneity, and comradeship but also brings everyone onto an equal level regardless of other class or identity traits that exist beyond the scope of the liminal moment.

The theoretical concept of communitas is highly relevant to experiences of sex consumption due to the timeworn notion of sex, whether transactional or recreational, as an inherent part of the journey to manhood. In tribal societies, the common thread was – and still is – an experience that involved emotional and physical pain and required a boy to pass the test of manhood: to show courage, endurance, and the ability to control one's emotions. These rituals were also commonly defined by sexual training: from lessons about sex and sexuality (Sotewu, 2016) to the duty to perform unprotected sex as an initiation experience (Hauchard, 2017) and the general encouragement to have sex (Hauchard, 2017; Munthali et al., 2004). While in Western societies, these initial trials are much more subtle and scarce, the consumption of commercial sex as the "dramatic acting" (Gilmore, 1990, p. 12) of a "rite of passage" serves as a manhood act, namely, a performance of hegemonic, heteronormative masculinity which marked men as "normal." At the same time, paying for sex is an essentially liminal and isolated experience found on the interstices of structure and the margins of social life due to the double standard that characterizes society's gaze. The social expectation that men have multiple and various sexual encounters to prove their heteronormative masculinity alongside the silence and public ostracism directed at commercial sex results in the delegitimization, whether explicit or implicit, of sharing such an experience publicly. It therefore leaves online communities as the only option for sharing commercial sexual experiences while forging "cultural intimacy" (Herzfeld, 2005) in the form of camaraderie communitas.

Herzfeld defined cultural intimacy as "the recognition of those aspects of a cultural identity that are considered a source of external embarrassment but that nevertheless provide insiders with their assurance of common sociality" (2005, p. 7). To illustrate this, he gave the example of Israeli bluntness that offers citizens a sense of defiant pride in the face of a more formal or official morality and, sometimes, of official disapproval. While Herzfeld used this term as part of his critical anthropological theorization of the bureaucratic nation-state and the process of constituting national identity, I found this theoretical concept extremely relevant for understanding the source of sex consumers' attraction to online communities where they can share their sexual experiences. Due to its stigmatized nature, sex consumption is often a source of embarrassment, intensified by the constant fear, even if only imagined, of outsiders' gaze penetrating the intimate space. Hence, in an atmosphere of fearing the breach of intimacy and the exposure of the "public secret" (Taussig, 1999), i.e., what is generally known but cannot, for one reason or another, be easily articulated, the online community is obsessively preoccupied with how to forge intimacy while securing the public secret in its boundaries.

One way of dealing with this constant fear and creating inner and collective cultural intimacy is to summon writing conventions as a symbolic bond. As previously mentioned, consuming paid sex is most often a solitary experience. Sharing and displaying it via sexual stories in front of like-minded peers thus becomes a communal ceremonial ritual – a "rite of passage" in itself that can only be displayed anonymously and in community secrecy. Furthermore, due to this inherent anonymity, social strata, such as race, class, ethnicity, religion, and age, have no meaning; everyone is on an allegedly equal level, allowing this liminal "moment" to become a safe space for all those perceived by society as "morally incorrect subjects" (Stoczkowski, 2008, p. 349). As such, writing sexual stories enables men to maneuver between the coercive power of society that perceives them as deviant and the respectable status they aspire to hold.

In this way, instead of being a purely informative feature, writing about sexual experiences becomes a "sacred" component: a communal and cultural practice of intimacy which uses rhetorical and metaphorical idioms that reflect one's familiar national character-building blocks.

The consumer/*freier*, the hunter/militarized subject, and the addict/victim are thus idioms of Israeli national identity. Moreover, for Israeli sex consumer communities, writing about sexual experiences has become an ethical rule of conduct: the ethic of individual sacrifice for the greater good of one's fellow community members. This resonates with both universal masculine camaraderie components and the local configuration of Israeli national character, which demands the individual to constantly sacrifice himself to the (Jewish) collective. As I have discussed elsewhere (Lahav-Raz, 2019), writing as the intimate act of transforming the individual sexual act into a public display has a range of objectives. Beyond merely soliciting recommendations, writing serves as a form of covert competition for ranking and thus increasing one's capital value. Writing has also become a stimulating practice in itself that aims to increase sexual arousal and thrill in both the writer and the reader. Finally, the emphasis on writing conventions (such as discussions about what the content of a "good" sexual report should be and an emphasis on the importance of proper punctuation and proofreading before publicizing) and adherence to the same metaphorical language is more than just the result of imitating intra-community norms.

These overly used rhetorical metaphors in the form of the consumer/*freier*, hunter/militarized subject, and addict/victim aim to cope with the fear of potential embarrassment. By rudimentarily structuring this unstructured liminal moment, communitext produces two levels of cultural intimacy: the first is cultural intimacy as sex consumers in the face of an outside world that regards them as immoral subjects, while the second is cultural intimacy as Israelis, especially when consuming sex abroad where they are compelled to maintain national honor. The communitext thus gains meaning by deconstructing the normative moral order and turning it into the ultimate vision of a culture in the eyes of sex consumers. However, as Turner (1969) showed, liminality and communitas are of the now: they are usually temporary, spontaneous, structurally defined, and limited, thus dialectically serving to reaffirm the existing social order. Hence, leaving the "public secret" inside community boundaries creates a sense of cultural intimacy and, thus, momentary relief while also reinforcing the fear that the public secret will exude outside community boundaries. As a result, it paradoxically maintains the consumption of paid sex as a hidden immoral activity that reaffirms the social structure of public condemnation.

I conclude this book by emphasizing the power of communitext and its ability to serve as an analytical thinking tool for future research on sex consumers' online communities. Beyond its ability to create momentary communitas characterized by a sense of belonging, togetherness, equality, and solidarity, and thus create cultural intimacy, the communitext holds threefold power. By combining sexual script theory and communitas, I argue that the communitext contains both Simon and Gagnon's (1986) three interwoven dimensions of cultural, interpersonal, and intrapsychic sexual scripts and Turner's (1969) three types of communitas. Simon and Gagnon (1986) showed how cultural norms and values influence both interpersonal and intrapsychic scripts; one's sexual motivations and sexual interactions are thus driven by cultural norms and values. Turner (1969) defined three types of communitas: (a) spontaneous communitas – the transient personal experience of togetherness which occurs during a counter-culture happening; (b) normative communitas – the transformation of communitas from its spontaneous state to a permanent social system which occurs due to the need for social control; and (c) ideological communitas – which can be applied to many utopian social models.

The communitext's first power is its role as the post-modern confessional. When the sex consumer shares via a public sexual story his sexual motivations and fantasies, what arouses him, and how he gives meaning to his sexual behavior – namely, all the integral elements of the intrapsychic sexual script – spontaneous communitas occurs. By sharing these sexual experiences, one can feel temporarily liberated and morally relieved from social ostracism.

The communitext's second power is as a habitat for new consumers. Writing, reading, and sharing sexual experiences serve as an instrumental apparatus for learning operation modes and the inner norms of the sex industry in the form of interpersonal interactions. Moreover, when the communitext becomes an "intellectual incubator" that teaches newcomers community and cultural norms, it moves from the spontaneous communitas to the normative communitas, namely, an organized and ideologized social system. As Asad (2018) claimed, language is not only what we do with it but also what it does to and in us; in the words of Heidegger, "language speaks" (1971, p. 971). Hence, communal rhetorical metaphors, based on many of the same categories, impact the individual sex consumer and his multiplicity of social ties. They define the insider and the outsider and divide the private from the public.

Finally, the communitext's third power is being one of the most significant players in the sex industry today. It extends the ability of consumers to communicate with sex workers and exchange information with each other about sexual services. At the same time, the communitext can pose various risks. These can manifest in destroying a sex worker's business by uploading negative, rude, or even defamatory reviews, thus contributing to sex workers' objectification, dehumanization, and stigmatization. Beyond the potentials and the risks, one cannot ignore the fact that, as a "collaborative project" (Kaplan & Haenlien, 2010), all players in the sex industry are aware of the everyday consumer power of sex consumers' online communities which not only reflects but also, predominantly, produces prevailing norms.

To conclude, this book has used the performative and theatrical nature of the three sexual scripts presented across the various chapters – the consumer, the hunter, and the addict – to illuminate the various dimensions of the contemporary male sexual experience in paid sexual interactions. I have shown that viewing the scripts not as a given set of rules but rather as fluid and flexible repertoires enables us to uncover the processes through which sexual scripts are reproduced and negotiated. These various cultural repertories mirror the interplay between one's inner world and one's intrinsic culture. Furthermore, since technology and consumerism are closely intertwined (Illouz, 2007), sex consumption cannot be understood today without turning the gaze toward digital technologies and their ability to allow sex consumers to release and negotiate the "public secret" (Taussig, 1999) of consuming paid sex. This book has therefore highlighted the use of digital technologies as a platform on which momentary communitas emerge as proof of their powerful impact on the rearrangement of modern-day sexual consumption and production. Under the triangular power of communitext, sex consumers can channel their intense feelings of social togetherness and belonging to create a localized form of homosociality and brotherhood which turns sex workers into a conduit through which these bonds are expressed. The communitext thus teaches us about the complex triangulation of cyberspace, capitalism, and consumerism in the sex industry and its close connection to emotional, social, and cultural logic.

Bibliography

Abd Abad, H. M. (2019). *"Traitors, snitches, collaborators": Analysing in-group criticism towards peace organisations in intractable conflict.* Master's Thesis in Peace and Conflict Studies, Department of Peace and Conflict Research. Uppsala University.

Adams, C. J. (2010). *The sexual politics of meat: A feminist-vegetarian critical theory* (rev. ed.). Continuum.

Adams-Santos, D. (2020). Sexuality and digital space. *Sociology Compass, 14*(8), e12818.

Agar, M. (1994). The intercultural frame. *International Journal of Intercultural Relations, 18*(2), 221–237.

Agustín, L. M. (2005). New research directions: The cultural study of commercial sex. *Sexualities, 8*(5), 618–631.

Agustín, L. M. (2007). Introduction to the cultural study of commercial sex: guest editor. *Sexualities, 10*(4), 403–407.

Agustín, L. M. (2008). *Sex at the margins: Migration, labour markets and the rescue industry.* Bloomsbury Publishing.

Almog, S. (2016). Israel, where prostitution is legal, debates criminalising the men who pay for sex. *The Conversation.*

Amir, D. (2008). Expulsion from the paradise of the gaze: Reflections on shame. *Theory and Criticism, 32,* 185–188 (Hebrew).

Amir, D., & Amir, M. (2004). The politics of prostitution and trafficking of women in Israel. In J. Outshoorn (Ed.), *The politics of prostitution: Women's movements, democratic states, and the globalization of commerce* (pp. 144–164). Cambridge University Press.

Androutsopoulos, J., & Beißwenger, M. (2008). Introduction: Data and methods in computer-mediated discourse analysis. *Language@ Internet, 5*(2). https://www.languageatinternet.org/articles/2008/1609

Appel, A. (2021). Connectionwork: "Connection" in the practices and perspectives of Israeli neoforagers. *HAU: Journal of Ethnographic Theory, 11*(2), 551–566.

Armengol, J. M. (2020). Performing manhood through animal killings? Revisions of hunting as a performance of masculinity in Ernest Hemingway's late writings. *Men and Masculinities, 23*(5), 833–851.

Asad, T. (2018). *Secular translations: Nation-state, modern self, and calculative reason.* Columbia University Press.

Avieli, N. (2011). Dog meat politics in a Vietnamese town. *Ethnology: An International Journal of Cultural and Social Anthropology, 50*(1), 59–78.

Avieli, N. (2013). Grilled nationalism: Power, masculinity and space in Israeli barbeques. *Food, Culture and Society, 16*(2), 301–320.

Avieli, N. (2018). *Food and power: A culinary ethnography of Israel* (Vol. 67). University of California Press.

Avieli, N., & Grosglik, R. (2013). Food and power in the Middle East and the Mediterranean: Practical concerns, theoretical considerations. *Food, Culture and Society, 16*(2), 181–195.

Bar-Tal, D. (2007). Sociopsychological foundations of intractable conflicts. *American Behavioral Scientist, 50*(11), 1430–1453.

Bar-Tal, D., Chernyak-Hai, L., Schori, N., & Gundar, A. (2009). A sense of self-perceived collective victimhood in intractable conflicts. *International Review of the Red Cross, 91*(874), 229–258.

Bauman, Z. (2013). *Liquid modernity*. John Wiley & Sons.

Ben-Ari, E., & Levi-Schreiber, E. (2000). Bodybuilding, character-building, and nationbuilding: Gender and military service in Israel. *Studies in Contemporary Judaism, 16*, 171–190.

Berdychevsky, L., & Nimrod, G. (2017). Sex as leisure in later life: A netnographic approach. *Leisure Sciences, 39*(3), 224–243. https://doi.org/10.1080/01490400.2016.1189368.

Berger, R. J., & Quinney, R. (2004). The narrative turn in social inquiry: Toward a storytelling sociology. In *Annual Meeting of the American Sociological Association*. http://www. allacademic. com/meta/p108465_index. Html.

Bergs, A. (2006). Analyzing online communication from a social network point of view: Questions, problems, perspectives. *Language@ Internet, 3*(3). https://www.languageatinternet.org/articles/2006/371

Bernstein, E. (2001). The meaning of the purchase: Desire, demand and the commerce of sex. *Ethnography, 2*(3), 389–420. https://doi.org/10.1177/14661380122230975.

Bernstein, E. (2007). *Temporarily yours: Intimacy, authenticity, and the commerce of sex*. The University of Chicago Press.

Bertone, C., & Ferrero-Camoletto, R. (2019). Beyond the client: Exploring men's sexual scripting. In M.-L. Skilbrei & M. Spanger (Eds.), *Understanding sex for sale: Meanings and moralities of sexual commerce* (pp. 96–111). Routledge.

Birch, P. (2015). *Why men buy sex: Examining sex worker clients*. Routledge.

Birenbaum-Carmeli, D., & Inhorn, M. C. (2009). Masculinity and marginality: Palestinian men's struggles with infertility in Israel and Lebanon. *Journal of Middle East Women's Studies, 5*(2), 23–52.

Blevins, K. R., & Holt, T. J. (2009). Examining the virtual subculture of johns. *Journal of Contemporary Ethnography, 38*(5), 619–648.

Bloch, L. R. (1998). Communicating as an American immigrant in Israel: The *freier* phenomenon and the pursuit of an alternative value system. *Research on Language and Social Interaction, 31*(2), 177–208.

Bloch, L. R. (2003). Who's afraid of being a *freier*? The analysis of communication through a key cultural frame. *Communication Theory, 13*, 125–159.

Bloch, L. R., & Lemish, D. (2005). "I know I'm a Freierit, but...": How a key cultural frame (en) genders a discourse of inequality. *Journal of Communication, 55*(1), 38–55.

Boltanski, L., & Thévenot, L. (1999). The sociology of critical capacity. *European Journal of Social Theory, 2*(3), 359–377.

Boltanski, L., & Thévenot, L. (2006). *On justification: Economies of worth*. Princeton University Press.

Boyarin, D. (1997). *Unheroic conduct: The rise of heterosexuality and the invention of the Jewish man*. University of California.

Boyd, D. (2008). How can qualitative Internet researchers define the boundaries of their projects: A response to Christine Hine. In A. Markham & N. Baym (Eds.), *Internet inquiry: Conversations about method* (pp. 26–32). Sage.

Brandth, B., & Haugen, M. S. (2006). Changing masculinity in a changing rural industry: Representations in the forestry press. In H. Campbell, M. Bell, & M. Finney (Eds.), *Country boys: Masculinity and rural life* (pp. 217–233). Penn State Press.

Brents, B. G. (2016). Neoliberalism's market morality and heteroflexibility: Protectionist and free market discourses in debates for legal prostitution. *Sexuality Research and Social Policy, 13*(4), 402–416.

Brents, B. G., & Hausbeck, K. (2007). Marketing sex: U.S. legal brothels and late capitalist consumption. *Sexualities, 10*(4), 425–439. https://doi.org/10.1177/1363460707080976.

Bridges, T., & Pascoe, C. J. (2014). Hybrid masculinities: New directions in the sociology of men and masculinities. *Sociology Compass, 8*(3), 246–258.

Bruker, G., & Sa'ar, A. (2019). In search of a lost masculinity: Israeli male sex tourists in Thailand. *Israeli Sociology, 20*(1), 50–73 (Hebrew).

Brooks-Gordon, B. (2006). *The price of sex: Prostitution, policy and society*. Willan.

Brooks-Gordon, B., & Gelsthorpe, L. (2003). What men say when apprehended for kerb crawling: A model of prostitutes clients' talk. *Psychology, Crime and Law, 9*(2), 145–171.

Browder, L. (2009). *Her best shot: Women and guns in America*. UNC Press.

Buerkle, C. W. (2009). Metrosexuality can stuff it: Beef consumption as (heteromasculine) fortification. *Text and Performance Quarterly, 29*(1), 77–93.

Burghart, K. O. (2018). What's on sale? A discourse analysis of four distinctive online escort advertisement websites. *Sexuality and Culture, 22*(1), 316–335.

Bye, L. M. (2003). Masculinity and rurality at play in stories about hunting. *Norsk Geografisk Tidsskrift – Norwegian Journal of Geography, 57*(3), 145–153.

Caldas-Coulthard, C. R. (1993). From discourse analysis to critical discourse analysis: The differential re-presentation of women and men speaking in written news. *Techniques of Description: Spoken and written discourse, 5*(2), 196–208.

Castle, T., & Lee, J. (2008). Ordering sex in cyberspace: A content analysis of escort websites. *International Journal of Cultural Studies, 11*(1), 107–121.

Charmaz, K. (2000). Grounded theory: Objectivist and constructivist methods. *Handbook of Qualitative Research, 2*(1), 509–535.

Chen, M.-H. (2017). Crossing borders to buy sex: Taiwanese men negotiating gender, class and nationality in the Chinese sex industry. *Sexualities, 20*(8), 921–942.

Chu, C. S. K., & Laidler, K. J. (2016). Becoming a male client of compensated dating. *Deviant Behavior, 37*(1), 47–65.

Colosi, R. (2022). 'I'm just with the guys and we're having a laugh': Exploring normative masculinity in a lap-dancing club setting, as a heteronormative space. *Sexualities, 25*(3), 222–241.

Cohen-Shalev, A. (2019). Between taming and training: The cinematic "Frier" as a long-distance runner. *Studies in Education, 17*(19), 255–239 (Hebrew).

Connell, R. (1995). *Masculinities*. Polity.

Connell, R. W. (1996). Teaching the boys: New research on masculinity, and gender strategies for schools. *Teachers College Record, 98*(2), 206–235.

Connell, R. W. (2005). Globalization, imperialism, and masculinities. In M. S. Kimmel, J. Hearn, & R. W. Connell (Eds.), *Handbook of studies on men and masculinities* (pp. 71–89). Sage Publication.

Connell, R. W. (2009). A thousand miles from kind: Men, masculinities and modern institutions. *The Journal of Men's Studies, 16*(3), 237–252.

Connell, R. W., & Messerschmidt, J. W. (2005). Hegemonic masculinity-Rethinking the concept. *Gender and Society, 19*(6), 829–859.

Cowen, N., & Colosi, R. (2020). Sex work and online platforms: What should regulation do? *Journal of Entrepreneurship and Public Policy, 10*(2), 284–303.

Cunningham, S., et al. (2017). Behind the screen: Commercial sex, digital spaces and working online. *Technology in Society, 53*, 47–54.

Coy, M., Smiley, C., & Tyler, M. (2019). Challenging the "prostitution problem": Dissenting voices, sex buyers, and the myth of neutrality in prostitution research. *Archives of Sexual Behavior, 48*(7), 1931–1935.

Davidson, J. O. C. (1998). *Prostitution, power, and freedom.* University of Michigan Press.

Davies, K., & Evans, L. (2007). A virtual view of managing violence among British escorts. *Deviant Behavior, 28*(6), 525–551.

Della Giusta, M., Di Tommaso, M. L., & Jewell, S. L. (2017). Men buying sex. Differences between urban and rural areas in the UK. *Urban Studies, 54*(3), 713–729.

Demetriou, D. Z. (2001). Connell's concept of hegemonic masculinity: A critique. *Theory and Society, 30*(3), 337–361.

Di Guardo, M. C., & Castriotta, M. (2014). The challenge and opportunities of crowdsourcing web communities: An Italian case study. *International Journal of Electronic Commerce Studies, 4*(1), 79–92.

Duffy, B. E., & Meisner, C. (2023). Platform governance at the margins: Social media creators' experiences with algorithmic (in) visibility. *Media, Culture and Society, 45*(2), 285–304.

Duvall, J. N. (1991). Doe hunting and masculinity: Song of Solomon and G. Down, Moses. *Arizona Quarterly: A Journal of American Literature, Culture, and Theory, 47*(1), 95–115.

Earle, S., & Sharp, K. (2008). Sex on the net: Online relations between the men who pay for sex. In S. Holland (Ed.), *Remote relationships in a small world* (Vol. 41, pp. 262–271). Peter Lang.

Earle, S., & Sharp, K. (2013). Intimacy, pleasure and the men who pay for sex. In G. Letherby, K. Williams, P. Birch, & M. E. Cain (Eds.), *Sex as crime?* (pp. 85–101). Routledge.

Earle, S., & Sharp, K. (2016). *Sex in cyberspace: Men who pay for sex.* Routledge.

Echols, A. (2016). Retrospective: Tangled up in pleasure and danger. *Signs: Journal of Women in Culture and Society, 42*(1), 11–22.

Fine, L. M. (2000). Rights of men, rights of passage: Hunting and masculinity at Leo Motors of Lansing, Michigan, 1945–1975. *Journal of Social History, 33*(4), 805–823.

Frank, K. (2003a). "Just trying to relax": Masculinity, masculinizing practices, and strip club regulars. *Journal of Sex Research, 40*(1), 61–75.

Frank, K. (2003b). *G-strings and sympathy: Strip club regulars and male desire.* Duke University Press.

Frank, K. (2005). Exploring the motivations and fantasies of strip club customers in relation to legal regulations. *Archives of Sexual Behavior, 34*(5), 487–504.

Gagnon, J. H. (1990). The explicit and implicit use of the scripting perspective in sex research. *Annual Review of Sex Research, 1*(1), 1–43.

Gagnon, J. H, & Simon, W. (1973). *Sexual conduct: The social sources of human sexuality.* Aldine.

Gal, D., & Wilkie, J. (2010). Real men don't eat quiche: Regulation of gender-expressive choices by men. *Social Psychological and Personality Science, 1*(4), 291–301.

Gavriely-Nuri, D. (2010). The idiosyncratic language of Israeli 'peace': A cultural approach to critical discourse analysis (CCDA). *Discourse and Society, 21*(5), 565–585.

Geertz, C. (1973). *The interpretation of cultures* (Vol. 5043). Basic books.

Gelfer, J. (2013). Meat and masculinity in men's ministries. *The Journal of Men's Studies, 21*(1), 78–91.

Gilroy, C., & Kashyap, R. (2021). Digital traces of sexualities: Understanding the salience of sexual identity through disclosure on social media. *Socius, 7*, 23780231211029499.

Gilmore, D. D. (1990). *Manhood in the making: Cultural concepts of masculinity.* Yale University Press.

Gilmore, D. D. (1997). *The hegemonic male: Masculinity in Portuguese town.* Berghahn Books.

Gluzman, M. (1997). The Zionist body: Nationalism and sexuality in Herzl's Altneuland. *Theory and Criticism, 11*, 145–162 (Hebrew).

Goffman, E. (1963). *Stigma: Notes on the management of spoiled identity.* Simon & Schuster.

Grazian, D. (2007). The girl hunt: Urban nightlife and the performance of masculinity as collective activity. *Symbolic Interaction, 30*(2), 221–243.

Grenz, S. (2005). Intersections of sex and power in research on prostitution: A female researcher interviewing male heterosexual clients. *Signs: Journal of Women in Culture and Society, 30*(4), 2091–2113.

Grosglik, R., & Lerner, J. (2021). Gastro-emotivism: How MasterChef Israel produces therapeutic collective belongings. *European Journal of Cultural Studies, 24*(5), 1053–1070.

Hakak, Y. (2009). Haredi male bodies in the public sphere: Negotiating with the religious text and secular Israeli men. *Journal of Men, Masculinities and Spirituality, 3*(2), 100–122.

Hallagan, D. (2012). Patriarchy and militarism. *Verbum, 10*(1), 53–58.

Halley, J., Kotiswaran, P., Shamir, H., & Thomas, C. (2006). From the international to the local in feminist legal responses to rape, prostitution/sex work, and sex trafficking: Four studies in contemporary governance feminism. *Harvard Journal of Law & Gender, 29*, 335.

Hamilton, C., & Denniss, R. (2005). *Affluenza: When too much is never enough.* Allen & Unwin.

Hammond, N. (2015). Men who pay for sex and the sex work movement? Client responses to stigma and increased regulation of commercial sex policy. *Social Policy and Society, 14*(1), 93–102.

Hammond, N., & van Hooff, J. (2020). "This Is Me, This Is What I Am, I Am a Man": The masculinities of men who pay for sex with women. *The Journal of Sex Research, 57*(5), 650–663.

Hardy, K. (2013). Equal to any other, but not the same as any other: The politics of sexual labour, the body and intercorporeality. In C. Wolkowitz, R. Cohen, T. Sanders, & K. Hardy (Eds.), *Body/sex work: Intimate, embodied and sexualised labour* (pp. 43–58). Palgrave Macmillan.

Hardy, K., & Barbagallo, C. (2021). Hustling the platform: Capitalist experiments and resistance in the digital sex industry. *South Atlantic Quarterly, 120*(3), 533–551.

Harrington, C. (2018). Gender policy models and calls to "tackle demand" for sex workers. *Sexuality Research and Social Policy, 15*(3), 249–258.

Hauchard, A. (2017). In Malawi, the horrors of a sexual initiation camp for young girls. *Le Monde*, 18 August 2017. Available: https://www.worldcrunch.com/culture -society/in-malawi-the-horrors-of-a-sexual-initiation-camp-foryoung-girls

Hazan, H. (2008). "And they shall not be ashamed": Conditions shame absence. *Theory and Criticism, 32*, 254–274 (Hebrew).

Heartfield, J. (2002). There is no masculinity crisis. *Genders, 35*(2), 1–15.

Heidegger, Martin (1971). *On the way to language*. San Francisco: Harper & Row.

Hertzog, E., & Lev, A. (2019). Male dominance under threat: Machoism confronts female defiance in Israeli gyms. *Journal of Contemporary Ethnography, 48*(6), 836–866.

Herzfeld, M. (2005). *Cultural intimacy: Social poetics in the nation-state*. Psychology Press.

Hirsch, D., & Kachtan, D. G. (2018). Is "hegemonic masculinity" hegemonic as masculinity? Two Israeli case studies. *Men and Masculinities, 21*(5), 687–708.

Holt, T. J., & Blevins, K. R. (2007). Examining sex work from the client's perspective: Assessing johns using on-line data. *Deviant Behavior, 28*(4), 333–354.

Holt, T. J., Blevins, K. R., & Kuhns, J. B. (2008). Examining the displacement practices of johns with on-line data. *Journal of Criminal Justice, 36*(6), 522–528.

Horswill, A., & Weitzer, R. (2018). Becoming a client: The socialization of novice buyers of sexual services. *Deviant Behavior, 39*(2), 148–158.

Huff, A. D. (2011). Buying the girlfriend experience: An exploration of the consumption experiences of male customers of escorts. In *Research in Consumer Behavior, 13*, 11–126.

Hughes, D. M. (2004). Prostitution online. *Journal of Trauma Practice, 2*(3–4), 115–131.

Huschke, S., & Schubotz, D. (2016). Commercial sex, clients, and Christian morals: Paying for sex in Ireland. *Sexualities, 19*(7), 869–887.

Huysamen, M. (2020). "There's massive pressure to please her": On the discursive production of men's desire to pay for sex. *The Journal of Sex Research, 57*(5), 639–649.

Huysamen, M., & Boonzaier, F. (2015). Men's constructions of masculinity and male sexuality through talk of buying sex. *Culture, Health and Sexuality, 17*(5), 541–554.

Huysamen, M., & Boonzaier, F. (2018). "Out of Africa": Racist discourse in men's talk on sex work. *Psychology in Society, 57*, 58–80.

Illouz, E. (2007). *Cold intimacies: The making of emotional capitalism*. Polity Press.

Illouz, E. (2008). *Saving the modern soul: Therapy, emotions, and the culture of self-help*. University of California Press.

Israeli, Z., & Rosman-Stollman, E. (2015). Men and boys: Representations of Israeli combat soldiers in the media. *Israel Studies Review, 30*(1), 66–85.

Itulua-Abumere, F. (2013). Understanding men and masculinity in modern society. *Open Journal of Social Science Research, 1*(2), 42–45.

Jones, A. (2015). Sex work in a digital era. *Sociology Compass, 9*(7), 558–570.

Jones, Z., & Hannem, S. (2018). Escort clients' sexual scripts and constructions of intimacy in commodified sexual relationships. *Symbolic Interaction, 41*(4), 488–512.

Joseph, L. J., & Black, P. (2012). Who's the man? Fragile masculinities, consumer masculinities, and the profiles of sex work clients. *Men and Masculinities, 15*(5), 486–506.

Kachtan, D., & Wasserman, V. (2015). (Un) dressing masculinity: The body as a site of ethno-gendered resistance. *Organization, 22*(3), 390–417.

Kamir, O. (2011). Zionism, masculinity, and feminism: Can they co-exist? In M. Shilo & G. Katz (Eds.), *Studies in the revival of Israel* (pp. 443–470). The Ben Gurion Reasearch Institute.

Kaneh-Shalit, T. (2017). "The Goal Is Not to Cheer You Up": Empathetic care in Israeli life coaching. *Ethos, 45*(1), 98–115.

Kaplan, D. (2003). *Brothers and others in arms: The making of love and war in Israeli combat units.* Psychology Press.

Kaplan, D. (2007). Folk models of dyadic male bonds in Israeli culture. *The Sociological Quarterly, 48*(1), 47–72.

Kaplan, D. (2008). Commemorating a suspended death: Missing soldiers and national solidarity in Israel. *American Ethnologist, 35*(3), 413–427.

Kaplan, A. M., & Haenlein, M. (2010). Users of the world, unite! The challenges and opportunities of Social Media. *Business Horizons, 53*(1), 59–68.

Kaplan, D., & Knoll, E. (2019). A cultural model of parenthood as engineering: How caregiving fathers construct a gender-neutral view of the parent role. *Journal of Family Issues, 40*(3), 363–389.

Karniel, Y. (2005, October 28). Why don't Israelis stand in line? *Alaxon.* https://alaxon .co.il/?p=74394.

Katriel, T. (1986). *Talking straight: Dugri speech in Israeli Sabra culture.* Cambridge University Press.

Katriel, T. (2020). *Defiant discourse: Speech and action in Grassroots Activism.* Routledge.

Katsulis, Y. (2010). "Living like a king": Conspicuous consumption, virtual communities, and the social construction of paid sexual encounters by US sex tourists. *Men and Masculinities, 13*(2), 210–230.

Kepten, A. (2023). The "supermen" club: Organizational secrecy and masculine identity in an Israeli national security organization. *Armed Forces and Society, 49*(2), 330–349.

Kheel, M. (2007). *Nature ethics: An ecofeminist perspective.* Rowman & Littlefield Publishers.

Kidron, C. A. (2010). Embracing the lived memory of genocide: Holocaust survivor and descendant renegade memory work at the House of Being. *American Ethnologist, 37*(3), 429–451.

Kimmel, M., Zinn, M. B., Hondagneu-Sotelo, P., Messner, M. A., & Denissen, A. M. (2013). Manufacturing rage: The cultural construction of aggrieved entitlement. In M. Kimmel (Ed.), *Angry white men: American masculinity at the end of an era* (pp. 31–68). Hachette.

Kingston, S., & Thomas, T. (2019). No model in practice: A 'Nordic model to respond to prostitution? *Crime, Law and Social Change*, *71*(4), 423–439.

Kong, T. S. (2015). Romancing the boundary: Client masculinities in the Chinese sex industry. *Culture, Health and Sexuality*, *17*(7), 810–824.

Kong, T. S. (2016). Buying sex as edgework: Hong Kong male clients in commercial sex. *British Journal of Criminology*, *56*(1), 105–122.

Kotsadam, A., & Jakobsson, N. (2011). Do laws affect attitudes? An assessment of the Norwegian prostitution law using longitudinal data. *International Review of Law and Economics*, *31*(2), 103–115.

Lahav-Raz, Y. (2019). The prosumer economy and the sex industry: The creation of an online community of sex prosumers. *Journal of Cultural Economy*, *12*(6), 539–551.

Lahav-Raz, Y. (2020a). "Hunting on the streets": Masculine repertoires among Israeli clients of street-based sex work. *Sexuality and Culture*, *24*(1), 230–247.

Lahav-Raz, Y. (2020b). Narrative struggles in online arenas: The Facebook feminist sex wars on the Israeli sex industry. *Feminist Media Studies*, *20*(6), 784–800.

Lahav-Raz, Y. (2022). The "addict sexual script": Addiction discourse among Israeli sex industry consumers. *Sexualities*, *25*(8), 987–1005.

Lahav-Raz, Y., Prior, A., & Peled, E. (2023). The question of moral worth in a controversial market: Moral justification regimes and boundary work among Israeli men who pay for sex abroad. *The Journal of Sex Research*, 1–12.

Lahav-Raz, Y., Prior, A., Shilo, G., & Peled, E. (2022). Helping individuals in the sex trade during COVID-19: The perspectives of Israeli aid organizations. *American Journal of Orthopsychiatry*, *92*(2), 168.

Lakoff, G., & Johnson, M. (1980). *Metaphors we live by*. University of Chicago Press.

Lamont, M. (2009). *The dignity of working men: Morality and the boundaries of race, class, and immigration*. Harvard University Press.

Lamont, M. (2012). Toward a comparative sociology of valuation and evaluation. *Annual Review of Sociology*, *38*(1), 201–221. https://doi.org/10.1146/annurev-soc -070308-120022

Lamont, M., & Mizrachi, N. (2012). Ordinary people doing extraordinary things: Responses to stigmatization in comparative perspective. *Ethnic and Racial Studies*, *35*(3), 365–381.

Lamont, M., & Thévenot, L. (2000). Introduction: Toward a renewed comparative cultural sociology. In M. Lamont & L. Thévenot (Eds.), *Rethinking comparative cultural sociology* (pp. 1–25). Cambridge University Press.

Lee, K. J., Dunlap, R., & Edwards, M. B. (2014). The implication of Bourdieu's Theory of Practice for leisure studies. *Leisure Sciences*, *36*(3), 314–323.

Levy, M., Hollander, E., & Noy-Canyon, S. (2016). The construction of Israeli 'masculinity' in the sports arena. *Israel Affairs*, *22*(2), 549–567.

Levy-Aronovic, S., Lahav-Raz, Y., & Raz, A. (2021). Who takes part in the political game? The sex work governance debate in Israel. *Sexuality Research and Social Policy*, *18*(3), 516–526.

Liepe-Levinson, K. (2003). *Strip show: Performances of gender and desire*. Routledge.

Lim, S. J., & Cheah, S. X. (2020). Do you know how to Cheong? Neutralization techniques adopted by new clients of sex workers. *Sexologies*, *29*(1), e1–e9.

Lindemann, D. J., Doggett, A., & Getsis, S. (2022). Hunting in a hostile climate?: Hegemonic masculinity and emphasized femininity on a hunting message board. *Men and Masculinities*, *25*(4), 602–621.

Littlefield, J. (2010). Men on the hunt: Ecofeminist insights into masculinity. *Marketing Theory, 10*(1), 97–117.

Littlefield, J., & Ozanne, J. L. (2009). Consumer socialization: The role of hunting and gun rituals in becoming a man. *Advances in Consumer Research, 36*, 634–635.

Livnat, Z. (2022). Speaking like an Israeli: Theory and practice. *Israel Studies in Language and Society, 15*, 37–73.

Lomsky-Feder, E. (2004). Life stories, war, and veterans: On the social distribution of memories. *Ethos, 32*(1), 82–109.

Lomsky-Feder, E., & Ben-Ari, E. (2007). Trauma, therapy and responsibility: Psychology and war in contemporary Israel. In A. Rao, M. Bollig, & M. Böck (Eds.), *The practice of war: Production, reproduction, and communication of armed violence* (pp. 111–131). Berghahn Books.

Lomsky-Feder, E., & Rapoport, T. (2003). Juggling models of masculinity: Russian-Jewish immigrants in the Israeli army. *Sociological Inquiry, 73*(1), 114–137.

Loo, T. (2001). Of moose and men: Hunting for masculinities in British Columbia, 1880–1939. *Western Historical Quarterly, 32*(3), 296–319.

Luke, B. (1998). Violent love: Hunting, heterosexuality, and the erotics of men's predation. *Feminist Studies, 24*(3), 627–655.

Mandelbaum, M. M. (2012). The "National Left" in Israeli public discourse: A critique. *Journal of Language and Politics, 11*(3), 448–467.

Mânsson, S. A. (1995). International prostitution and traffic in persons from a Swedish perspective. In *Combating traffic in persons. Proceedings of the conference on traffic in persons, held from 15–19 November 1994 in Utrecht and Maastricht. SIM Special No* (pp. 109–124). SIM.

Marttila, A. M. (2008). Desiring the 'other': Prostitution clients on a transnational red-light district in the border area of Finland, Estonia and Russia. *Gender, Technology and Development, 12*(1), 31–51.

Masters, N. T., Casey, E., Wells, E. A., & Morrison, D. M. (2013). Sexual scripts among young heterosexually active men and women: Continuity and change. *Journal of Sex Research, 50*(5), 409–420.

Mbonye, M., Siu, G., & Seeley, J. (2022). Conflicted masculinities: Understanding dilemmas and (re) configurations of masculinity among men in long-term relationships with female sex workers, in Kampala, Uganda. *Culture, Health and Sexuality, 24*(6), 856–869.

McGarry, K., & FitzGerald, S. (2018). Introduction: Social justice through and Agenda for Change. In S. A. FitzGerald & K. McGarry (Eds.), *Realising justice for sex workers: An agenda for change* (pp. xv–xxxv). Rowman & Littlefield International.

McKenzie, C. (2000). The British big-game hunting tradition, masculinity and fraternalism with particular reference to the 'the shikar club'. *Sports Historian, 20*(1), 70–96.

McKenzie, C. (2005). "Sadly neglected": Hunting and gendered identities: A study in gender construction. *The International Journal of the History of Sport, 22*(4), 545–562.

McLean, K. E. (2021). 'Post-crisis masculinities' in Sierra Leone: Revisiting masculinity theory. *Gender, Place and Culture, 28*(6), 786–805.

Messner, M. A. (1997). *Politics of masculinities: Men in movements.* Altamira Press.

Milrod, C., & Monto, M. A. (2012). The hobbyist and the girlfriend experience: Behaviors and preferences of male customers of internet sexual service providers. *Deviant Behavior, 33*(10), 792–810.

Milrod, C., & Monto, M. (2017). Older male clients of female sex workers in the United States. *Archives of Sexual Behavior, 46*(6), 1867–1876.

Milrod, C., & Weitzer, R. (2012). The intimacy prism emotion management among the clients of escorts. *Men and Masculinities, 15*(5), 447–467.

Monterescu, D. (2003). Stranger masculinities: Cultural construction of Arab maleness in Jaffa. *Israeli Sociology, 5,* 121–159 (Hebrew).

Monto, M. A. (2000). Why men seek out prostitutes. In R. Weitzer (Ed.), *Sex for sale: Prostitution, pornography, and the sex industry* (pp. 67–83). Routledge.

Monto, M. A., & McRee, N. (2005). A comparison of the male customers of female street prostitutes with national samples of men. *International Journal of Offender Therapy and Comparative Criminology, 49*(5), 505–529.

Monto, M. A., & Milrod, C. (2014). Ordinary or peculiar men? Comparing the customers of prostitutes with a nationally representative sample of men. *International Journal of Offender Therapy and Comparative Criminology, 58*(7), 802–820.

Munthali, A., Chimbiri, A., & Zulu, E. (2004). *Adolescent sexual and reproductive health in Malawi: A synthesis of research evidence.* Occasional Report No. 15. The Alan Guttmacher Institute.

Nath, J. (2011). Gendered fare? A qualitative investigation of alternative food and masculinities. *Journal of Sociology, 47*(3), 261–278.

Neal, M. (2018). Dirty customers: Stigma and identity among sex tourists. *Journal of Consumer Culture, 18*(1), 131–148.

Nuran, E. R. O. L. (2015). The role of narrative methods in sociology: Stories as a powerful tool to understand individual and society. *Sosyoloji Araştırmaları Dergisi, 18*(1), 103–125.

Nurse, A. (2015). *Policing wildlife: Perspectives on the enforcement of wildlife legislation.* Springer.

Offer, S., & Kaplan, D. (2021). The "new father" between ideals and practices: New masculinity ideology, gender role attitudes, and fathers' involvement in childcare. *Social Problems, 68*(4), 986–1009.

Ompad, D. C., Bell, D. L., Amesty, S., Nyitray, A. G., Papenfuss, M., Lazcano-Ponce, E., Villa, L. L., & Giuliano, A. R. (2013). Men who purchase sex, who are they? An interurban comparison. *Journal of Urban Health, 90*(6), 1166–1180.

Ortner, S. B. (1973). On key symbols. *American Anthropologist, 75*(5), 1338–1346.

Oselin, S. S., & Weitzer, R. (2013). Organizations working on behalf of prostitutes: An analysis of goals, practices, and strategies. *Sexualities, 16*(3–4), 445–466.

Pajnik, M., Kambouri, N., Renault, M., & Šori, I. (2016). Digitalising sex commerce and sex work: A comparative analysis of French, Greek and Slovenian websites. *Gender, Place and Culture, 23*(3), 345–364.

Paltrinieri, R., & Esposti, P. D. (2013). Processes of inclusion and exclusion in the sphere of prosumerism. *Future Internet, 5*(1), 21–33.

Parasecoli, F. (2005). Feeding hard bodies: Food and masculinities in men's fitness magazines. *Food and Foodways, 13*(1–2), 17–37.

Parry, J. (2010). Gender and slaughter in popular gastronomy. *Feminism and Psychology, 20*(3), 381–396.

Peled, E., Shilo, G., Marton Marom, Y., & Eick, U. (2020). The attitudes toward men who pay for sex scale: Development and preliminary validation. *Archives of Sexual Behavior, 49*(8), 3075–3087.

Peng, Y. W. (2007). Buying sex: Domination and difference in the discourses of Taiwanese Piao-ke. *Men and Masculinities, 9*(3), 315–336.

Perlman, Y. (2021). "You'd better run: There is no place for sport hunting in Israel!" *Walla!* https://travel.walla.co.il/item/3458107.

Pettinger, L. (2011). 'Knows how to please a man': Studying customers to understand service work. *The Sociological Review, 59*(2), 223–241.

Pettinger, L. (2013). Market moralities in the field of commercial sex. *Journal of Cultural Economy, 6*(2), 184–199.

Pettinger, L. (2015). The judgement machine: Markets, internet technologies and policies in commercial sex. *Social Policy and Society, 14*(1), 135–143.

Pitcher, J. (2015). Sex work and modes of self-employment in the informal economy: Diverse business practices and constraints to effective working. *Social Policy and Society, 14*(1), 113–123.

Pitcher, J. (2019). Intimate labour and the state: Contrasting policy discourses with the working experiences of indoor sex workers. *Sexuality Research and Social Policy, 16*(2), 138–150.

Pitts, M. K., Smith, A. M., Grierson, J., O'Brien, M., & Misson, S. (2004). Who pays for sex and why? An analysis of social and motivational factors associated with male clients of sex workers. *Archives of Sexual Behavior, 33*(4), 353–358.

Plummer, K. (2002). *Telling sexual stories: Power, change and social worlds.* Routledge.

Potts, A., & Parry, J. (2010). Vegan sexuality: Challenging heteronormative masculinity through meat-free sex. *Feminism and Psychology, 20*(1), 53–72.

Presser, L., & Taylor, W. V. (2011). An autoethnography of hunting. *Crime, Law and Social Change, 55*(5), 483–494.

Prior, A. (2022). Paying for sex during COVID-19 pandemic: The experiences of Israeli men. *Sexuality Research and Social Policy, 19*(1), 50–62.

Prior, A., & Peled, E. (2019). Paying for sex while traveling as tourists: The experiences of Israeli men. *The Journal of Sex Research, 56*(4–5), 659–669.

Prior, A., & Peled, E. (2021). Identity construction of men who pay women for sex: A qualitative meta-synthesis. *The Journal of Sex Research, 58*(6), 724–742.

Prior, A., & Peled, E. (2022). Gendered power relations in women-to-men interviews on controversial sexual behavior. *International Journal of Social Research Methodology, 25*(3), 277–291.

Ram, U. (2013). *The globalization of Israel: Mcworld in Tel Aviv, jihad in Jerusalem.* Routledge.

Rand, H. M. (2022). 'As straight as they come': Expressions of masculinities within digital sex markets. *Sexualities*, 1–16.

Rissel, C., Donovan, B., Yeung, A., de Visser, R. O., Grulich, A., Simpson, J. M., & Richters, J. (2017). Decriminalization of sex work is not associated with more men paying for sex: Results from the second Australian study of health and relationships. *Sexuality Research and Social Policy, 14*(1), 81–86.

Ritzer, G., & Jurgenson, N. (2010). Production, consumption, prosumption: The nature of capitalism in the age of the digital 'prosumer'. *Journal of Consumer Culture, 10*(1), 13–36.

Robinson, S. (2000). *Marked men: White masculinity in crisis.* Columbia University Press.

Rogers, R. A. (2007). From hunting magic to shamanism: Interpretations of Native American rock art and the contemporary crisis in masculinity. *Women's Studies in Communication, 30*(1), 78–110.

Roniger, L., & Feige, M. (1992). From pioneer to Freier: The changing models of generalized exchange in Israel. *European Journal of Sociology/Archives Européennes De Sociologie, 33*(2), 280–307.

Roniger, L., & Feige, M. (1993). "The Freier culture and Israeli identity". *Alpaim, 7*, 118–136 (Hebrew).

Rozin, P., Hormes, J. M., Faith, M. S., & Wansink, B. (2012). Is meat male? A quantitative multimethod framework to establish metaphoric relationships. *Journal of Consumer Research, 39*(3), 629–643.

Rosenmann, A., Kaplan, D., Gaunt, R., Pinho, M., & Guy, M. (2018). Consumer masculinity ideology: Conceptualization and initial findings on men's emerging body concerns. *Psychology of Men and Masculinity, 19*(2), 257.

Rosenthal, R. (2005). *The comprehensive slang dictionary*. Keter (Hebrew).

Rubin, G. S. (2002). Thinking sex: Notes for a radical theory of the politics of sexuality. In P. Aggleton & R. Parker (Eds.), *Culture, society and sexuality a reader* (pp. 143–178). Routledge.

Ruby, M. B., & Heine, S. J. (2011). Meat, morals, and masculinity. *Appetite, 56*(2), 447–450.

Sa'ar, A., & Yahia-Younis, T. (2008). Masculinity in crisis: The case of Palestinians in Israel. *British Journal of Middle Eastern Studies, 35*(3), 305–323.

Sanders, T. (2005). Researching the online sex work community. In C. Hine (Ed.), *Virtual methods: Issues in social research on the internet* (pp. 67–79). Berg.

Sanders, T. (2008). Male sexual scripts: Intimacy, sexuality and pleasure in the purchase of commercial sex. *Sociology, 42*(3), 400–417.

Sanders, T. (2013). *Paying for pleasure: Men who buy sex*. Willan Routledge.

Sanders, T. (2018). Unpacking the process of destigmatization of sex work/ers: Response to Weitzer 'Resistance to sex work stigma'. *Sexualities, 21*(5–6), 736–739.

Sanders, T., Brents, B. G., & Wakefield, C. (2020). *Paying for sex in a digital age: US and UK perspectives*. Routledge.

Sanders, T., & Campbell, R. (2014). Criminalization, protection and rights: Global tensions in the governance of commercial sex. *Criminology and Criminal Justice, 14*(5), 535–548.

Sanders, T., Connelly, L., & King, L. J. (2016). On our own terms: The working conditions of internet-based sex workers in the UK. *Sociological Research Online, 21*(4), 133–146.

Sanders, T., O'Neill, M., & Pitcher, J. (2017). *Prostitution: Sex work, policy & politics*. Sage.

Sanders, T., Scoular, J., Campbell, R., Pitcher, J., & Cunningham, S. (2018). *Internet sex work: Beyond the gaze*. Springer International Publishing.

Sasson-Levy, O. (2002). Constructing identities at the margins: Masculinities and citizenship in the Israeli army. *Sociological Quarterly, 43*(3), 357–383.

Sasson-Levy, O. (2003). Military, masculinity, and citizenship: Tensions and contradictions in the experience of blue-collar soldiers. *Identities: Global Studies in Culture and Power, 10*(3), 319–345.

Sasson-Levy, O. (2008). Individual bodies, collective state interests: The case of Israeli combat soldiers. *Men and Masculinities, 10*(3), 296–321.

Santo, Y., Carmeli, A., & Rahav, G. (2016). The national survey on the phenomenon of prostitution in Israel. *Israel (Hebrew): The Ministry of Social Affairs and Social Services and the Ministry of Public Security.*

Scheibling, C., & Lafrance, M. (2019). Man up but stay smooth: Hybrid masculinities in advertising for men's grooming products. *The Journal of Men's Studies, 27*(2), 222–239.

Schori-Eyal, N., Halperin, E., & Bar-Tal, D. (2014). Three layers of collective victimhood: Effects of multileveled victimhood on intergroup conflicts in the Israeli–Arab context. *Journal of Applied Social Psychology, 44*(12), 778–794.

Schwarz, O. (2010). Going to bed with a camera: On the visualization of sexuality and the production of knowledge. *International Journal of Cultural Studies, 13*(6), 637–656.

Seltenreich, Y. (2009). Masculinity, respect and body in the PJCA settlements of the galilee during the settlement period. *Israeli Sociology, 1,* 137–157 (Hebrew).

Shilo, G., Peled, E., & Shamir, H. (2020). *Paying for sex, receiving payment for sex and attitudes towards prostitution/sex Work policy and the law prohibiting the purchase of sexual services: Data from a survey of the Israeli Jewish population.* Tel-Aviv University (Hebrew).

Shilo, G., Gewirtz-Meydan, A., & Peled, E. (2021). Men who pay for sex once, more than once, or not at all: The associations between attitudes toward paying for sex, socio-demographic characteristics, and frequency of sex payment. *The Journal of Sex Research, 58*(6), 754–762.

Shilo, G., & Mor, Z. (2020). Sexual practices and risk behaviors of Israeli adult heterosexual men. *AIDS Care, 32*(5), 567–571.

Shilon, Y, (Producer, Director) (2008). *Rumors [documentary film].*

Showalter, E. (1981). Feminist criticism in the wilderness. *Critical Inquiry, 8*(2), 179–205.

Shumka, L., Strega, S., & Hallgrimsdottir, H. K. (2017). "I wanted to feel like a man again": Hegemonic masculinity in relation to the purchase of street-level sex. *Frontiers in Sociology, 2,* 15.

Simon, W., & Gagnon, J. H. (1986). Sexual scripts: Permanence and change. *Archives of Sexual Behavior, 15*(2), 97–120.

Sinha, M. (2008). Triangular erotics: The politics of masculinity, imperialism and big-game hunting in Rider Haggard's She. *Critical Survey, 20*(3), 29–43.

Sion, L., & Ben-Ari, E. (2009). Imagined masculinity: Body, sexuality, and family among Israeli military reserves. *Symbolic Interaction, 32*(1), 21–43.

Smalley, A. L. (2005). 'I just like to kill things': Women, men and the gender of sport hunting in the United States, 1940–1973. *Gender and History, 17*(1), 183–209.

Smith, M., & Mac, J. (2018). *Revolting prostitutes: The fight for sex workers' rights.* Verso Books.

Sobal, J. (2005). Men, meat, and marriage: Models of masculinity. *Food and Foodways, 13*(1–2), 135–158.

Sollund, R. (2020). Wildlife crime: A crime of hegemonic masculinity? *Social Sciences, 9*(6), 93.

Sotewu, S. S. (2016). A visual narrative reflecting on upbringing of Xhosa girls with special reference to "intonjane". Unpublished Master's dissertation. Rhodes University, South Africa.

Spector-Mersel, G., & Gilbar, O. (2021). From military masculinity toward hybrid masculinities: Constructing a new sense of manhood among veterans treated for PTSS. *Men and Masculinities, 24*(5), 862–883.

Spender, D. (1985). *Man made language.* Routledge.

Soothill, K., & Sanders, T. (2005). The geographical mobility, preferences and pleasures of prolific punters: A demonstration study of the activities of prostitutes' clients. *Sociological Research Online, 10*(1), 17–30.

Sramek, J. (2006). "Face Him like a Briton": Tiger hunting, imperialism, and British masculinity in colonial India, 1800–1875. *Victorian Studies, 48*(4), 659–680.

Sterling, A., Van Der Meulen, E., & Meulen, V. E. (2018). "We are not criminals": Sex work clients in Canada and the constitution of risk knowledge. *Canadian Journal of Law and Society, 33*(3), 291–308.

Stibbe, A. (2004). Health and the social construction of masculinity in men's health magazine. *Men and Masculinities, 7*(1), 31–51.

Stoczkowski, W. (2008). The "fourth AIM" of anthropology. *Anthropological Theory, 8*(4), 345–356.

Stommel, W. (2008). Conversation analysis and community of practice as approaches to studying online community. *Language@ Internet, 5*(5). https://www.languageatinternet.org/articles/2008/1537

Strauss, A., & Corbin, J. (1994). Grounded theory methodology: An overview. In N. K. Denzin & Y. S. Lincoln (Eds.), *Handbook of qualitative research* (pp. 273–285). Sage Publications, Inc.

Suler, J. (2004). The online disinhibition effect. *Cyberpsychology & behavior, 7*(3), 321–326.

Sumpter, K. C. (2015). Masculinity and meat consumption: An analysis through the theoretical lens of hegemonic masculinity and alternative masculinity theories. *Sociology Compass, 9*(2), 104–114.

Swidler, A. (1986). Culture in action: Symbols and strategies. *American Sociological Review, 51*(2), 273–286.

Swords, J., Laing, M., & Cook, I. R. (2023). Platforms, sex work and their interconnectedness. *Sexualities, 26*(3), 277–297.

Tal-Hadar, R., Prior, A., & Peled, E. (2022). How perceptions of masculinity and intimate sexual relationships shape men's experiences of paying for sex: A qualitative exploration. *Sexualities*, 13634607221137314.

Talmon, M. (2001). *Blues for the Lost Sabra: Groups and nostalgia in Israeli cinema.* The Open University (Hebrew).

Taussig, M. T. (1999). *Defacement: Public secrecy and the labor of the negative.* Stanford University Press.

Tiidenberg, K., & Van Der Nagel, E. (2020). *Sex and social media.* Emerald Group Publishing.

Turner, V. (1969). *The ritual process: Structure and anti-structure.* Chicago Publishing.

Turner, V. (1974). Liminal to liminoid, in play, flow, and ritual: An essay in comparative symbology. *Rice Institute Pamphlet-Rice University Studies, 60*(3), 53–92.

Toffler, A. (1980). *The third wave: The classic study of tomorrow.* Bantan Books.

Tyler, M. (2004). Managing between the sheets: Lifestyle magazines and the management of sexuality in everyday life. *Sexualities, 7*(1), 81–106.

Tyler, M., & Jovanovski, N. (2018). The limits of ethical consumption in the sex industry: An analysis of online brothel reviews. *Women's Studies International Forum, 66*, 9–16.

Vaughn, M. P. (2019). Client power and the sex work transaction: The influence of race, class, and sex work role in the post-apartheid sex work industry. *Sexuality and Culture, 23*(3), 826–847.

Velthuis, O., & van Doorn, N. (2020). Weathering winner-take-all: How rankings constitute competition on webcam sex platforms, and what performers can do about it. In D. Stark (Ed.), *The performance complex: Competition and competitions in social life* (pp. 167–186). Oxford University Press.

Vuolajärvi, N. (2019). Governing in the name of caring—The Nordic model of prostitution and its punitive consequences for migrants who sell sex. *Sexuality Research and Social Policy*, *16*(2), 151–165.

Waltman, M. (2011). Prohibiting sex purchasing and ending trafficking: The Swedish prostitution law. *Michigan Journal of International Law*, *33*, 133.

Ward, H., Mercer, C. H., Wellings, K., Fenton, K., Erens, B., Copas, A., & Johnson, A. M. (2005). Who pays for sex? An analysis of the increasing prevalence of female commercial sex contacts among men in Britain. *Sexually Transmitted Infections*, *81*(6), 467–471.

Wasserman, V., Dayan, I., & Ben-Ari, E. (2018). Upgraded masculinity: A gendered analysis of the debriefing in the Israeli air force. *Gender and Society*, *32*(2), 228–251.

Waxman, D. (2016). Is Israeli democracy in danger? *Current History*, *115*(785), 360–362.

Weitzer, R. (2000). Deficiencies in the sociology of sex work. *Sociology of Crime, Law, and Deviance*, *2*, 259–279.

Weitzer, R. (2007). The social construction of sex trafficking: Ideology and institutionalization of a moral crusade. *Politics and Society*, *35*(3), 447–475.

Weitzer, R. (2009). Sociology of sex work. *Annual Review of Sociology*, *35*(1), 213–234.

Weitzer, R. (2013). Researching sex work in the twenty-first century. *Contemporary Sociology: A Journal of Reviews*, *42*(5), 713–722.

Weitzer, R. (2018). Resistance to sex work stigma. *Sexualities*, *21*(5–6), 717–729.

Weitzer, R. (2020). The campaign against sex work in the United States: A successful moral crusade. *Sexuality Research and Social Policy*, *17*(3), 399–414.

Yair, G. (2011). *The code of Israeliness: The Ten Commandments for the twenty-first century*. Keter (Hebrew).

Yair, G. (2014). Israeli existential anxiety: Cultural trauma and the constitution of national character. *Social Identities*, *20*(4–5), 346–362.

Zerubavel, Y. (2002). The "Mythological Sabra" and Jewish past: trauma, memory, and contested identities. *Israel Studies*, *7*(2), 115–144.

Zheng, T. (2006). Cool masculinity: Male clients' sex consumption and business alliance in urban China's sex industry. *Journal of Contemporary China*, *15*(46), 161–182.

Index

For Product Safety Concerns and Information please contact our EU
representative GPSR@taylorandfrancis.com
Taylor & Francis Verlag GmbH, Kaufingerstraße 24, 80331 München, Germany

www.ingramcontent.com/pod-product-compliance
Lightning Source LLC
Chambersburg PA
CBHW071056280326
41928CB00050B/2532

9 780367 652722